RED SKY AT NIGHT

RED SKY AT NIGHT

Communism Confronts Christianity
in China

by

LESLIE T. LYALL

HODDER AND STOUGHTON

Printed in Great Britain for Hodder and Stoughton Limited
St. Paul's House, Warwick Lane, London, E.C.4 by
Hazell Watson & Viney Ltd, Aylesbury, Bucks

"When it is evening ye say, It will be fair weather: for the sky is red..."

AUTHOR'S PREFACE

"HISTORY is bunk!" is not what Henry Ford said. What he really said was "History as usually taught is bunk!" Certainly, history which depends on spicy anecdotes and apocryphal stories for interest and history which is told with a bias to suit the presuppositions or political theory of the historian is not true history.

Instead of the mechanical interpretation of history on which Marxists base their theories, the true meaning of history lies in the unfolding drama of God's stupendous purpose for mankind—the tragedy of human sin, the devastation it has wrought and the epic record of redemption. The Old Testament prophets interpreted current events in the light of God's will and purpose, and in so doing, laid down principles for interpreting the meaning of all history, in which the sovereign activity of an almighty and all-wise God is to be recognised. Herbert Butterfield, former Professor of Modern History at Cambridge University, sees history in this light—the outworking of the Divine moral law in the affairs of men, the effects of man's sin and the inevitable retribution which sin causes.

In the Garden of Eden, God Himself indicated the future course of history as a result of man's sin in the words addressed to Satan : "I will put enmity between thee and the woman and between thy seed and her seed; it shall bruise thy head and thou shalt bruise his heel." History thus becomes the stage for the unfolding story of the age-long conflict between God's elect people and the God-rejecting followers of Satan. The climax of this conflict was reached at Calvary when Christ, the seed of the woman, was crucified but Satan received a mortal wound.

The Book of Revelation takes up the theme. In vivid

imagery the inspired author foretells the continuing conflict between the Church and Satan. The reader shares the
foreboding and sorrow of the writer when no one could
open the sealed book of history, and rejoices with the elders
when the Lamb that was slain is declared worthy to open
the seals of the book. For Christ alone is the Lord of history
and the author of redemption. He reigns from His throne
above the troubled seas of human life. History, which to the
uninitiated is a meaningless tangled skein, is in fact an
orderly progress towards its glorious consummation when
Christ, the Lion of Judah, will reign as King of kings and
Lord of lords over all the world.

China, with its unbroken national history of three or
four thousand years, is not excluded from the Divine plan.
Four major attempts have been made to take the Gospel to
China—in the seventh, the thirteenth, the sixteenth and
the nineteenth centuries. The last was the most prolonged
and the most concentrated, but was brought to an end by
the Communist seizure of power. The concluding words of
my previous book, *Come Wind, Come Weather*, written in
1959, were : "Faith sees beyond the present darkness to a
new dawn for the Church in China. ... The present dusk is
not the dusk of day's end, but the dusk that precedes the
dawn." Another decade has gone by during which the
organised Church in China has been brought to the point of
extinction. But, paradoxically enough, this situation and
the events leading to it have kindled hopes all over the
world that the day may not be far distant when the long
siege of God's Church in China will be lifted and outside
relief will speed to her aid. It may not be American or
European aid. But it could be aid from hundreds of
Chinese, backed up by other Asians now training themselves in God's school of discipleship for this very purpose
and opportunity. No Christian can accept as final the idea
that God has written off one quarter of the human race and
destined them never to hear the Gospel. Nearly eight hundred million souls live in China—by far the greatest unevangelised segment of the world's population today. And
even though the door seems firmly closed now, our Sover-

eign Lord is the One of whom it is said, "He openeth and no man shutteth · and shutteth, and no man openeth."

Red Sky at Night has this hope of a brighter tomorrow written large across its pages. It outlines the historic developments over the past ten years and brings the story of the Chinese Church up to date. In response to a letter in *The Christian* in 1966, it attempts to explain simply for the man in the street the nature of Communism and suggests a Christian approach. The growing interest in student circles in Marxist and Maoist principles demands a more widespread understanding of the subject. Also to be found is a critical examination of missionary work in the past and some constructive suggestions for a desirable course of action should a return to China ever become possible. The writer's fervent hope is that this book will stimulate thought and discussion about the tremendous issues raised. But most of all it will fail in its purpose if it does not stimulate prayer—prayer which will increase in volume until the gates of brass give way and the teeming millions of China hear again of the only Saviour who died and rose that they might enjoy life abundant.

CONTENTS

	Author's Preface	6
I	A Kingdom Divided	11
II	A Church Goes into the Shadows	31
III	Bitter Lessons	45
IV	Brief Guide to Communism	53
V	A Deceptive Counterfeit	63
VI	Christ for the Marxist	73
VII	Unto Caesar	80
VIII	Criticism and Self-Criticism	89
IX	Return to China	97
X	Challenge of Communism	108
XI	Confrontation	115
	Appendix	117
	Bibliography	125
	Index	126

CHAPTER I

A KINGDOM DIVIDED

1965 was a year of destiny for Chairman Mao Tse-tung.

Seven years had gone by since the Great Leap Forward had been announced with a fanfare at the Party Congress in May, 1958. Immediately, the first experimental communes were created. These were to be the springboard for a great leap of economic progress and the entire nation braced itself for the effort.

But the pathway ahead was far from smooth; the 1959 rebellion in Tibet, ruthlessly suppressed with the death of sixty-five thousand Tibetans, cast sombre shadows. The following year the Soviet Union and the East European nations denounced China and ridiculed her commune experiments. Russia withdrew all her expert advisers, leaving China to paddle her own sampan. The emergence of Khruschev as Russia's leader was a turning point in Sino-Soviet relations which have steadily deteriorated ever since.

Great Leap Failure

During 1960 China's leaders were faced with the cruel truth that they had failed. Their agricultural policy had gone badly wrong. Grim reports of famine in some areas and severe food shortages everywhere swamped their early optimism. Red-faced officials who had reported doubled crops confessed to deception and in January 1961, Prime Minister Chou En-lai told Edgar Snow, the American journalist and long-time friend of Chairman Mao, that grain production in 1960, far from attaining new targets, had fallen below that of the previous two years. It was a bitter, bitter winter for China. Flood, drought and insect pests accentuated the failure, but the real blame for the grave situation was the monumental failure of the Administration and its economic policies. Relatives and friends of starving people on the mainland came to their aid on a vast scale; nearly twelve million food parcels were despatched from Hong Kong in 1961 and a similar number the following year. The flow of refugees to Hong Kong and Macao increased. In Shanghai, unrest burst out in posters openly blaming the Government for the repeated crop failures. Finally, to alleviate the food shortages, the Government was compelled to purchase large quantities of Canadian and Australian wheat with foreign currency which could ill be spared.

Revisionism

The disaster was above all a blow to Chairman Mao's personal prestige. He was a 'god that had failed'. The Mao mystique was shattered. The Great Leap Forward was his own brain child. He was now compelled by public sentiment to approve modifications in the strict commune system and to restore some degree of private property and enterprise. This 'economism' was repugnant to Mao since it smacked of 'revisionism'. The Minister of Defence, Marshal Peng Teh-huai, who at the Lushan Conference of the Communist Party in 1959 had opposed Mao, the communes, and especially the Great Leap Forward, and been dismissed, could now say 'I told you so!' Peng had, it is believed, the tacit support of Liu Shao-chi who, nevertheless, succeeded Mao as Chairman of the Republic (though not of the Party) at the end of 1958. Despite Liu's status, however, it was Marshal Lin Piao who remained the man closest to the Chairman of the Party, spiritually speaking.

But Mao had forfeited his reputation for infallibility and sections of the public hostile to him continued to hold 'revisionist' views. The angry Chairman displayed a growing impatience with these intellectuals, especially after 1962. To protect the younger generation from heresy, he launched the Socialist Education Movement and increased the pressures against a number of well-known writers and historians in the Party, including Wu Han the dramatist and deputy mayor of Peking, who interpreted the current situation in a way which reflected unfavourably on the Chairman.

Reform by Labour

A law requiring the rustication (*hsia fang*) of intellectuals had been passed in 1957. In 1960 millions of students were ordered to the rural communes to help overcome the crisis in agricultural production. In 1963 tens of thousands of civil servants, intellectuals and students again poured into the rural areas to experience a personal reformation of attitude and outlook in social relations by participating in farm labour. By the end of 1965 forty million youths and intellectuals were, reluctantly, employed in farm work. Most found the crude living conditions almost unbearable, while the peasants, on their part, resented their presence, and even derided the boasts made by the youthful white-collared urbanites.

The Question of the Succession

But in spite of one 'rectification' campaign after another, the influence of Mao's opponents in the Central Committee of the Party persisted : he repeatedly failed to gain the total control of the Party machinery which he sought. More drastic action than ever was called for if the future of the Chinese revolution was to be safeguarded.

Furthermore, the ageing leadership of the Party inspired a debate in the national Press about the necessity for ensuring "revolutionary successors who will not betray the revolution". Clearly a crisis was looming, largely over the problem of Chairman Mao's successor and the ensuring of the continuation of Mao's interpretation of Marxism-Leninism.

The Indonesian Débâcle

Despite internal problems of great magnitude China persistently engaged in exporting revolution. Following Mao's theories on 'people's wars', China was encouraging the Vietminh and the Vietcong in their fight for revolution in Vietnam. The situation along the Indian border was a deliberate threat to India. Burma, once China's friend, had now come to resent Chinese interference in her internal affairs and attempts to dominate Burmese politics. In Africa, Chinese

Communists were busily subverting one country after another, both training and arming rebel forces and exploiting
every favourable situation. "The East wind is prevailing
over the West wind" was an expression of confidence in the
coming success of world revolution.

But meanwhile the ripest opportunity appeared to be in
Asia—particularly in Indonesia where President Sukarno,
who had been welcomed in Peking and Moscow at different
times, was obviously well-disposed towards Communism provided that this could be adapted to Indonesian life and
tradition. His 'Nasakom' concept was intended to bring together in harmony the forces of nationalism, religion and
Communism. The Indonesian Communist Party was the
largest in any country outside the Communist world and in
firm control of the trades unions. Several senior ministers
were decidedly pro-Communist. Although Russia supplied
Indonesia with naval vessels and planes, China was the
more popular 'big brother' and actually attempted to ex-
clude Russian representation at the Afro-Asian Conference
at Bandung in 1955. China also encouraged and applauded
Indonesia's action in resigning her membership in the
United Nations. The Chinese and their Indonesian co-
conspirators were laying a carefully worked out plot to take
over Indonesia. How far President Sukarno was personally
involved is unknown, but fortunately the army was led by
anti-Communist generals. The attempted coup d'état took
place during the night of September 30th, 1965. Four generals were assassinated in their beds, but two miraculously
escaped, alerted the armed forces and so saved the country
from a Communist revolution.

The reaction against the Chinese and the Communists
took a violent form—'the revenge of the generals'. Hundreds of thousands of known Communists and their depen-
dants were massacred. Eventually the suspect President was
forced out of office and General Suharto, one of the sur-
vivors of the midnight assassination and the Commander-
in-Chief of the armed forces, was appointed in Sukarno's
place.

The humiliating failure of Mao's designs to grab the rich
prize of Indonesia's one hundred million people and their

immense potential wealth, following on the heels of the
catastrophic failure of the Great Leap Forward, sent Chairman Mao's prestige in the outside world tumbling yet lower.
Diplomatically he had received one setback after another
in Europe, Africa and in Asia. History may prove that the
Indonesian débâcle marked the beginning of the decline of
Communist power throughout Asia, as well as in China
itself. In November, Sino-Soviet relations reached a new
level of hostility. 1965, therefore, was a highly critical year
for the seventy-three-year-old leader, brooding in the
seclusion of his residence in Peking's lovely Western Hills.
He was at the crossroads of destiny. The tide of opposition at
home was running strongly against him. Vigorous and early
action to maintain support for his own leadership and for
his particular brand of Communism was imperative. Mao
was also genuinely concerned with posterity and with the
question as to who best would perpetuate his principles and
plans for world revolution.

The Cultural Revolution

In the autumn, therefore, as the leaves of the trees around
his home were turning red and gold, Mao, by-passing the
normal machinery, summoned a secret session of the Central Committee of the Party. Quickly he set up *ad hoc*
committees as a framework for the new and turbulent
chapter in China's history which was about to open—a
chapter fraught with grave dangers for China itself and for
the world. The Chairman was about to unleash the Great
Proletarian Cultural Revolution, his final gamble when
everything else had failed. He feared that Chinese society
was heading towards a slide into Soviet-style 'revisionism'.
Mao, who had never sincerely renounced the Stalinist theory
of intensified class struggle as society approaches the stage
of full Communism, was now preparing for fresh class
struggles and Stalinist-style purges. (Practically every military or civil official who has risen to prominence in the
People's Republic of China during the past eleven years
has either disappeared from public life or finds himself
under severe criticism now.) On November 10th, from
Shanghai, Chairman Mao sounded 'the clarion call for the

Great Proletarian Cultural Revolution', which was to 'touch people to their very souls'. At the same time he attacked Wu Han and his 'black gang' of writers in Peking, and thus indirectly Peng Chen, the mayor and the Peking Party Committee. Thereafter, for undisclosed reasons, Mao disappeared from the public view for six months.

The Maoists now engaged in a battle of words against the old line 'conservative' officials who opposed any tightening up or radicalisation in domestic policy. But their efforts were unsuccessful. Aware of the strength of the opposition he was facing, Mao had been planning to harness the ardent revolutionary youth of China to stem the tide of intellectual revisionism, to purge the 'intellectuals' of bourgeois tendencies and defeat counter-revolution within the Party itself.

On May 16th, Mao, now back in Peking, presided over a Central Committee meeting and on May 29th approved the organisation of the first Red Guard group connected with Tsinghua University. Others soon followed. On June 1st, seven students and cadres displayed the first 'big character poster' on the walls of Peking University, attacking the President, Lu Pang, and the university Party Committee. Two days later the Maoists regained control of the national *People's Daily*, purged the Peking Party Committee of 165 prominent, elderly members and removed Peng Chen and Wu Han from all their Party and Government posts. This was a first step toward purging the entire Party apparatus, nationwide and at all levels.

Peking University students had the honour of 'firing the first volley of guns' in the Great Proletarian Cultural Revolution. The student protesters were bent on the reform of the educational system. They censured the President of the University and by securing his dismissal, initiated a nationwide purge of university administration and intellectuals. The new draft educational curriculum gave central place to Mao's writings and 35 million sets of his selected works were printed for mass circulation. "We do not need brains! Our heads are armed with the ideas of Mao Tse-tung!" was a slogan which indicates the anti-intellectual character of the new paroxysm. *Pravda* had this to say: "The Red Guards have mastered the lesson that the main enemy of

Mao Tse-tung is he who tries to think." On June 16th all universities and high schools were ordered to close for six months so that the students could participate in the Cultural Revolution. It was to be nearly two years before many returned to the classroom.

On July 16th Chairman Mao, to dramatise the full-scale launching of the Revolution, (allegedly) launched his plump body into the swift-flowing current of the Yangtze River at Hankow to make his famous swim. The press presented to an incredulous world, photos of Mao's head bobbing like a cork amid other corks—his ardent admirers and fellow swimmers—in the muddy torrent. So Mao was not, after all, a sick man, as rumours persisted in claiming, but a leader full of vigour and ready to direct the most intensive rectification campaign so far undertaken in China!

Poster Debate

A feature of the Revolution from the beginning was the public debate in the form of 'big character posters' making charge and counter charge and publicising the latest slogans. Seas of red paper and oceans of ink were used to denounce 'revisionists' in vitriolic terms. This was a form of warfare in which the Chinese writing-brush was mightier than the sword. Day after day the acrimonious charges mounted in ferocity, one poster answering another. This public washing of the nation's dirty linen was felt essential to the new revolution, the most radical upheaval in Chinese education and culture ever devised. Indeed the whole thing was a gigantic ideological purge, from which nothing and nobody was immune. In November, even Liu Shao-Chi, Chairman of the Republic, already deprived of his real authority in August came under public attack. This 'top party person taking the capitalist road' was denounced as the 'Chinese Kruschev' and accused of consistently opposing the beloved leader Chairman Mao, of committing a series of towering crimes against the Party and the People, and of engineering the July-August revolts in South China. Marshal Teng Hsiao-ping, the Secretary General of the Party, was also accused. Chairman Liu's and Marshal Peng's crimes really

consisted in repeated attempts to restrain Mao in some
of his more extravagant schemes

The Red Guards

During the sweltering days of August, 1966, nine tumultu-
ous rallies of the newly formed 'Red Guards' astounded
even Peking, long since blasé about mass rallies. An aggre-
gate of fourteen million youths paraded outside the Tien An
(Heavenly Peace) Gate of the ancient Forbidden City,
where emperors once lived and reigned. Now it was Mao
who stood there with Marshal Lin Piao, his henchman and
heir-apparent, to witness the march past. The young people
had enshrined Mao as their hero : he was to them a celestial
deity quite beyond criticism. Statues of him had been
erected everywhere. His portrait gazed benignly down on
eight hundred million citizens from every conceivable van-
tage point. Postcards and calendars without Mao's portrait
were rare. In Shao-shan, Mao's birthplace near Changsha,
a painting of Mao showed him in white robes and sandals
with a rosy glow radiating from him. *Chairman Mao is the
Red Sun in our hearts* was the title of a documentary film
made to celebrate the seventeenth anniversary of the found-
ing of the People's Republic of China. His deification was
virtually complete. Reverently they bowed to his portraits.
"We love our great Party and great leader Chairman
Mao!" proclaimed the ubiquitous posters. The *Hung wei-
ping*, wearing armbands inscribed in Mao's own handwrit-
ing and Mao buttons on their blue boiler suits, were the
Chairman's new instrument to carry revolution to the people,
his chosen successors now to be given field experience in
revolution. They were to supersede the Party machinery
which Mao no longer trusted.

The Little Red Book

The 'Little Red Book' of *Quotations from the Thoughts
of Mao Tse-tung* is treated like a holy book—carried on the
person, studied first thing in the morning and last thing at
night, by individuals and in groups : the slogans are memor-
ised and applied to every activity of the day. 'Study the
works of Mao Tse-tung' was the national text for 1964 when

Mao's influence seemed to be on the wane. Mao's writings, it is claimed, combine "the original truth of Marxism-Leninism with the concrete practice of the Chinese Revolution." "Long live Mao Tse-tung's *Thoughts*!" They are the touchstone of orthodoxy and will, it is believed, outlive the Prophet himself. Every cadre must publicise them and travellers have seen them pasted up in every conceivable place, including children's prams and the harnesses of pack animals. They have displaced the lucky charms of an earlier superstitious age. An air hostess, trusting to the *Thoughts* of Mao, feels no need to use a seat-belt when taking off and landing. Athletes attribute their good performance to reliance on the *Thoughts*. Military strategy must depend on them. And Vice-Chairman Lin Piao stands second to Mao because he is "the closest comrade-in-arms, the best pupil of our great leader Chairman Mao, the one who holds highest the Great Red Banner of Mao Tse-tung's Thought, comprehends Mao Tse-tung's Thought most profoundly and applies it best."

Iconoclasm

The Cultural Revolution was directed against the 'four olds' : old customs, old habits, old cultures and old thoughts. For the most part teenagers, the Red Guards, liberated from their studies and instigated to 'make revolution', set about the task with fanatical enthusiasm. Mob rule now prevailed. In Peking persons wearing 'western' style clothing were ordered to wear simple dress, girls with 'Hong Kong' hair styles were denounced and taxis declared to be 'bourgeois luxuries'. Private homes were invaded and superfluous or too expensive furniture thrown out into the street. Physical violence became common and the traditional Chinese respect for age was abandoned. Elderly people endured public humiliation and were marched through the streets, sometimes naked. Being made to parade through the streets wearing a dunce's hat was one form of insult for individuals singled out for public disgrace. As far as they were permitted, the Red Guards smashed every *objet d'art* of Greek, Roman and Chinese 'bourgeois culture'. Museums were closed to the public. Only the People's Liberation

Army prevented the young hooligans from totally wrecking the Forbidden City and the Ming Tombs near Peking, priceless and beautiful monuments of China's past glory. Churches were closed and church leaders maltreated and humiliated. Bibles and religious books were searched out and destroyed.

Soon the activities, the insults and the vandalism of the Red Guards spread throughout China as one hundred million youths went on an ideological rampage, "like a roaring swift current sweeping across thousands of miles" (*Red Flag*, April 24th, 1967)—a "kind of nightmare Children's Crusade" against religion, against China's cultural heritage and especially against all suspected of anti-Mao sentiments. Violence increased as these arrogant teenagers, provided with free travel passes and possessed with travel mania, swarmed everywhere, disrupting communications and the normal life of the nation. Hundreds of thousands of those previously ordered out to work in the country (*hsia fang*) seized the opportunity of free trips back to the comforts of their city homes. Newspapers were forced to suspend publication temporarily. Following the public denunciation of Chairman Liu Shao-chi in November, in December mass action against the Party leadership was carried to the factories and the rural communes : even the Minister of Culture, a vice-premier, found himself dragged through the streets, and other leading figures in the Party were arrested. Such officially inspired anarchy and so massive a demonstration of student power are without historical parallel.

Man after Mao's Image

What was the Cultural Revolution intended to achieve? *The People's Daily* of June 8th, 1967 said : "We are critics of the old world . . . the old system of exploitation . . . the bourgeois scholars and authorities. In the movement of criticism now developing on an unprecedented scale, a great new era emerges on the horizon in which the seven hundred million people of China will be people of wisdom." Karl M . . . . amed of the emergence of a new society and a . . . . mankind in which human nature itself would . . . d. The long-range goal of the Cultural Revolution was therefore the remoulding of man and society, the creation of a new type of human being, the evolution of a 'future Communist man'. The ancient and deeply-rooted feudal characteristics of the nation would be replaced with qualities and ideals more suitable for leading a socialist state along the road to Communism. In a society reverting to selfishness and personal advantage, Mao sought to re-create the Yenan spirit of austerity, self-sacrifice and revolutionary zeal. The grand design was thus a new folk culture, a new ethic, a new personal faith based on Mao: in short, a new pseudo-religion. It was therefore essential to overhaul the higher educational system so that ideological training would in future be at its very centre. It is now clear that the Cultural Revolution had three aims: basically it was an ideological struggle against the economic policies of the revisionists; then it was a power struggle for leadership to determine the future course of the revolution and finally it was a mass youth movement with a puritanical desire to renew human nature by purging it of all wrong thinking, desires and habits. What went wrong?

Factionalism

The most confusing aspect of the situation in China developing out of the Cultural Revolution was the bewildering growth of 'factionalism'. Not a day went by in the early months of 1968 without some newspaper discussion of the major political phenomenon of mass factionalism. It is clear that Chairman Mao himself was astounded at the deep rifts his Cultural Revolution had torn in the fabric of Chinese political life.

The first Red Guard groups were organised by Maoists in 1966 by dissatisfied student activists eager to have a share in purging the Party apparatus of functionaries opposed to Mao. Throughout the year many more groups were formed until they embraced almost the entire high school and university student population. But inevitably, despite their common cause, there was inter-group rivalry which erupted from time to time in violence. Then the Maoists in Peking, frustrated at their failure to remove the senior Party offi-

cials, authorised the masses to overthrow their immediate
superiors and to 'seize power' for themselves A scramble
for power resulted among the rival groups. Alarmed, the
threatened officials, in self-defence, organised now adult
groups against the Red Guard reign of terror and the proli-
feration of contending factions created even greater chaos.
These revolutionary bodies were argumentative, ill-disci-
plined and ambitious. They called themselves by such names
as Spring Thunder, Ground Command, Doctrine Guards,
Red Banner, Revolutionary Rebels, Red Iron Fighters,
Grand Rebel Army, Alliance Command, East Wind, Proletarian Revolutionaries etc.

When the Cultural Revolution was extended to the farms
and factories early in 1967, the Revolutionary Rebels seized
power from the Shanghai Party and municipal authorities
in what is now called the 'January Revolution'. Workers
who had been enjoying the incentive benefits of 'economism'
feared for their livelihood if Maoist dogma took its place.
So they, too, organised groups to resist the high-handed Red
Guards. Labour discipline broke down and massive strikes
and industrial sabotage resulted. In Shanghai the port and
the railways were paralysed. Matters were getting out of
hand. The danger of 'anarchism' was publicly voiced.
Fighting broke out in widely separated regions. Over fifty
died and hundreds were wounded in clashes in Nanking.
The normal machinery of government could no longer cope
with the myriad contending 'mass organisations'. Just after
a siege of the Soviet embassy began on January 26th (was
not Russia the poisonous source of 'revisionism'?), Chairman Mao reluctantly decided to commit the People's
Liberation Army (P.L.A.) and issued his eight point direc-
tions. This decision, which destroyed the image of the Cultural Revolution as a spontaneous mass movement, was not a
popular one. But from January 1967 on, the P.L.A. assumed
an increasingly vital role. The 'mass organisations' now
began to look for allies among other groups. As smaller
groups coalesced, two huge opposing factional organisations,
still inwardly divided, emerged. The 'radical' coalition included the Red Guards and all who stood to gain in power
by a change in the *status quo*, while the 'conservative'

coalition was mainly composed of groups favouring a return to the pre-Cultural Revolution *status quo*. Both sides paid lip service to Mao, but when large-scale fighting between the heavily armed forces of the two coalitions broke out in August 1967, it began to look like full-scale civil war. The Army remained aloof though at times it had intervened to restrain the excessive violence of the cultural revolutionaries.

Government was becoming utterly chaotic. The more cautious leaders in Peking, therefore, persuaded 'Helmsman' Mao to steer the ship into calmer waters. Orders went out for the factional fighting to cease and for the Red Guards to return to their classrooms and lecture rooms to study Mao's works and the Cultural Revolution. But it was not until the spring of 1968 that most of the primary schoolers and half the middle schoolers were back at their desks. Perhaps Mao felt that many of the objectives of the campaign had been achieved—especially that of giving the younger generation a form of synthetic revolutionary experience. But he had certainly not eliminated all those who disagreed with his policies.

Three Way Alliances

The Red Guards were mostly youthful and inexperienced, but the release of their mass energies had been explosive and in the end highly dangerous. Their violence and the increasing internecine strife had disrupted the economy and threatened to cause another disaster on the scale of the Great Leap Forward. Spring sowing was hindered and the harvest was again threatened. High authorities in the capital, taking their courage in their hands, began to condemn Red Guard extremism and to warn the country of the dangers of anarchism. These attempts to curb the excesses were made by new bodies based on 'Three Way Alliances' viz., the revolutionary masses (Red Guards etc.), the revolutionary cadres (the old loyal Party officials), and the Army. *The People's Daily* actually rebuked over-zealous Maoists for 'leftist errors'.

In order to restore order and to curb the excesses of the revolutionaries Mao was compelled to turn again to the

People's Liberation Army, the only cohesive force left in the country. The Army's new active role was unpopular and caused much friction and heavy criticism. The long siege of the Soviet Embassy was lifted. Chou En-lai, the man between the extreme left and the extreme right, emerged more powerfully than ever as the key figure in the tragic drama when he sought to mediate between the opposing factions and to get the economy on its feet again.

Disillusionment

But it was easier to kindle the flames than to damp them down. The 'anti-imperialist' struggle overflowed to Hong Kong in May accompanied by violence and provocation. In August 1967 the British Legation in Peking was burned down. Throughout China armed clashes continued, compelling Mao himself to tour the country in September to ensure that factional fighting ceased. Students were ignoring his earlier instructions and most universities and schools remained closed; it was too humiliating for the students to accept reinstated teachers and lecturers, whom they had once denounced as revisionists; a stalemate resulted. Frustrated with failure to achieve their revolutionary aims, disappointed at the success of the Peking moderates and angry at being virtually cast aside, the Red Guards had no stomach for a return to the classroom. Factionalism and the breakdown of rule by law had resulted in crime, immorality and profiteering—black market activities being more prevalent than at any time since 1949. Premier Chou En-lai is reported to have complained that many students were opting out of the struggle completely and turning to "lovemaking, playing poker and leading a dissipated life". These are the 'wanderers', the 'hippies' of China, apathetic, afraid, disillusioned and their hopes of preferment shattered. The high degree of discipline and the public puritanism of earlier years was on the wane.

Foreign Guests

Amid the turmoil, Chairman Mao's 'Three Way Alliances' succeeded in setting up new Revolutionary Committees (i.e. 'seized power') in nine provinces during 1967.

This was some measure of victory for the greatly sobered leader. Thanks to the influence of the moderates who seemed to be consolidating their power at the centre, China appeared to be emerging from the chaos and the confusion which the Cultural Revolution had created.

A picture of life in China in early 1968 is provided by the experience of a group of fifty-seven Australians and New Zealanders who toured Canton, Shanghai, Peking, Hankow, Wuchang and Changsha. Their leader was an active Christian. For them it was the most intense, emotional and highly-charged experience of their lives. In Canton, their first stop, compulsory study of Mao's thoughts for hours on end was a mind-numbing experience. On their visit to schools, factories and communes, they were to hear some of the popular *Quotations* repeated again and again. Their 'Little Red Books' were already dog-eared before they proceeded on their journey.

At the time, the whole country was in such turmoil that the authorities were rather unhappy about entertaining tourists. The outcome of the anti-revisionist struggle was still in doubt. Judging by the outward evidence of the number of troops in the streets, things were probably at their worst during their visit to Wuhan where a Revolutionary Committee had only just been set up. In Shanghai and Peking, however, Revolutionary Committees had been set up long since. Changsha still had no such committee at the time of their visit. It was therefore risky to say ahead of time what cities could be safely visited and consequently the fifteen-man team of guides supplied by the China Travel Service lacked the usual confidence and efficiency of that organisation. The excitement of 1967, when some of the party had made a previous visit, had died down. Red Guards were no longer conspicuous in public and the once proudly-worn armband was rare in contrast to the situation before. But the Australian and New Zealand students, who stayed with Red Guards in the universities of Futan and Tungchi in Shanghai, found those at Futan very militant still.

In Shanghai the tour nearly came to a premature end when one of the Australians drew the peanut cartoon

character Snoopy, showing the dog leaping constantly into
the air with the 'balloon' reading 'Long live Chairman
Mao!' A Red Guard who saw it took a serious view of the
incident and a heated criticism and self-criticism session
took place before the tour could proceed. Later in the tour,
at Changsha, a picture postcard of Mao and a Mao button
with a hole burned through it were discovered in the waste
paper basket. Guards and hotel staff immediately crowded
into the room and an angry altercation ensued. While dis-
mayed at the personality cult of Mao and the severe restrictions on personal freedom, the students were impressed with
the experiment in mass politics — 'a massive exercise in
political education'. But the group was not able to meet a
single Christian or any one from the Religious Affairs
Bureau.

Revolutionary Committees

In the first four months of 1968, fourteen other provinces
set up their Revolutionary Committees, but in fact internal
harmony was entirely lacking and the earlier Revolutionary
Committees were not functioning smoothly. In late March
the Army Chief of Staff was purged, as factionalism spread
to the Army. The smouldering fires flared up again in the
spring and violence exceeding that of 1967 broke out all
over the country. The fading posters were torn down and
new ones began to appear with new and old targets for
abuse and criticism. New 'devils', 'ogres', 'monsters', 'appari-
tions' and 'spectres' were discovered and renewed stress laid
on loyalty to Mao, his Thoughts and his Line. The extrem-
ists had again seized control and chaos was exalted as a
virtue without which the concealed enemies of Mao could
not be exposed. Mao himself, however, was reported to have
wept at a five-hour meeting at his Peking residence as he
spoke of the grave difficulties besetting the nation. At this
meeting he threatened the extremist Red Guard group at
Peking University that unless they mended their ways, all
institutions of higher learning would be placed under military control. This confrontation served to highlight the
problem that Mao had created for himself and the nation
in mobilising student power to 'make revolution'. When,

alarmed by the consequences of his own actions, he tried to deprive the students of their power and force them back to their classrooms, he found many of them turning against him and his policies. So Mao finally appealed again to the workers. While hundreds of thousands of Red Guard 'intellectuals' were ordered to the country 'worker-peasant propaganda teams' were sent to the universities to put the young revolutionaries in their place and to 'tidy up the mess' of the Cultural Revolution by means of the 'struggle-criticism-transformation movement'. "The great army of the working class," according to Yao Wen-yuan in his epitaph of the Cultural Revolution titled 'The working class must exercise leadership in everything', "is marching into all educational institutions and is to occupy and lead them for ever." China's youth, three hundred million of whom are of student age, are the ultimate victims of the turmoil of the past three years.

Szechwan with its seventy million people and vast natural resources was, in traditional style, the most recalcitrant of the provinces. The powerful governor, who had opposed the extremism of the Cultural Revolution from the start, was deposed in May 1968 and was subsequently frequently paraded before mass denunciation rallies, 'pale and trembling'. But bloody fighting between rival factions did not stop and the governor's influence was not diminished. All the main cities were affected. On 31st May, however, a provincial Revolutionary Committee was finally established and hailed as a great victory. Now only five of the twenty-nine provinces remained without a Revolutionary Committee: Fukien (east China) Kwangsi (south China), Yunnan (southwest China), Tibet and Sinkiang (the north-west province and the centre of the nuclear factories)—all strategically important frontier areas.

May saw a grave uprising of factional violence right across the country with the worst features in Kwangsi. Wuchow was devastated by an extensive fire and bloodshed was on an appalling scale. The gruesome evidence of thousands of bound and mutilated corpses floating down the Pearl River, some being picked up in Hong Kong, was plain to the eyes of the world. The nationwide disruption of rail communications was worst at Liuchow, where supplies for Vietnam were held up. Everywhere the transport of coal and other essential commodities for industry was experiencing long delays. The Chinese economy in general was showing increasing signs of strain as a result of the total disruption of normal life and the severest floods of the century in south China.

Unable to solve the problem of setting up Revolutionary Committees by the masses locally, representatives of Fukien, Kwangsi, Yunnan, Tibet and Sinkiang met in Peking in August to negotiate a settlement. On the 13th, Yunnan accepted a Revolutionary Committee, and two days later hundreds of men, women and children were summoned again to parade through the streets of the capital to celebrate another great victory for Maoist leadership. Fukien followed on August 19th against violent opposition at home. On the 26th Kwangsi declared its own Revolutionary Committee, and on September 6th Revolutionary Committees were established in the last two remaining provinces—Tibet and Sinkiang. Peking celebrated again and a broadcast heralded the event as "the final victory of the Cultural Revolution". The 'victory' was completed in time to celebrate China's National Day on October 1st and a possible 9th Party Congress before the end of 1968. Nevertheless factional strife was continuing on a very large scale. The struggle was no longer one about policies but power. Political attacks on the Revolutionary Committees from without and fighting within prevented them from attaining any prestige or authority. Chairman Mao had been forced to postpone his Utopia-building by mass activists to devote himself to restoring order and authority with the strong support of the People's Liberation Army. By the Cultural Revolution he may have succeeded in weeding out and destroying the main elements within the Party hierarchy whom he regarded as most dangerous to his ideals. But the basic division between the 'Red' and 'Expert' schools of thought remains : shall political theories or practical policies and technical efficiency take precedence? This debate will continue for a long time and will certainly give rise to further strife and endless purges. Meanwhile the mystery of Liu Shao-chi,

'China's Khruschev', vilified but undeposed as Head of State, baffles explanation.

Liberalisation

After fifty years of Communist tyranny, the whole Communist world is seething with discontent. Khruschev led the fight against Stalinism and gave the Russians a taste of some measure of relaxation of inhuman laws and regulations. Yugoslavia had already led the way. The fever proved infectious. In January 1968, Czechoslovakia emerged joyfully from her years of darkness. The press, the radio, television and churches suddenly took full advantage of their freedom. The younger generation in Rumania declared themselves in full sympathy with these exciting developments. Poland, Bulgaria, Hungary and East Germany all developed symptoms of the infection. The hope was for 'Socialism with humanity'. But the old dogmatists of Russia became alarmed. Their definition of Communism takes the U.S.S.R. a long way back towards Stalinism. Could you have 'revisionists' and 'liberalising' policies without risking the ultimate destruction of Communism itself? Fearing the forces of change and using the bogey of 'counter-revolution', Russia defied the United Nations Charter and world opinion by the treacherous invasion and occupation of Czechoslovakia. The mask is off and Communism's real face is exposed. In its advance towards world domination, where will the forces of Communism attack next? Rumania, Israel, West Germany?

But the tide is turning. Eighty-eight Russian writers and intellectuals secretly condemned the treachery of their own country. For the young generation of the world it is 'Democratic socialism—yes! Tyrannical Communism—no!' The men in the Kremlin are frightened men. The seventy-six year old chairman Mao, following his two spectacular failures and a Pyrrhic victory in the Cultural Revolution, is clearly losing his grip. In April the Soviet press bitterly accused him of destroying the Communist movement in China. When Russia invaded Czechoslovakia, China replied by denouncing the invasion, though attacking the new Czech leadership at the same time. These events will undoubtedly strengthen his determination to resist all liberalisation in his own country. The question of Mao's successor and whether the Revolution will eventually take a new turn are certainly wide open. It seems unlikely that anyone of Mao's stature can be found to assume his position after his death. So while the Maoist era draws to a close, China faces a new transitional period. The leaders of the Chinese Communist Revolution are in deep trouble.

The Psalmist vividly describes (Psalm 2) the final revolt of man against God—the rulers taking counsel against the Lord to break away from Divine government. But the Sovereign Ruler of the world, looking down from His throne on the laughable though tragic postures of rebellious man, frustrates his designs. For God has entrusted to the risen Lord Jesus Christ the judgment of the nations and the final Kingship of the world. China, a kingdom divided against itself, cannot stand for long. Communism, because of its militant atheism, contains the seeds of its own disintegration and is doomed to ultimate destruction. For God rules and "blessed are all they that put their trust in Him".

CHAPTER II

A CHURCH GOES INTO THE SHADOWS

CHRISTMAS chimes were silent throughout China in 1967. No room was found for the Christ child in any Communist inn. Church buildings which once rang with the music of carols and *The Messiah* were boarded up or in use as schools and Red Guard halls. Scarlet 'big character posters' emblazoned the walls, the work of teenagers who had never seen a Christian missionary from overseas and thought that Jesus was just a famous Jew. The 'Jesus religion', like the 'Buddha religion', the 'Tao religion', the 'Confucius religion' and the 'Hui (Muslim) religion', was one of the 'four olds' which had to go. Chairman Mao Tse-tung had decreed it. So church buildings were closed, religious symbols removed and Christian homes systematically ransacked for Bibles and Christian literature—some many times. What was found was burned.

"If the foundations be destroyed," said David, "what can the righteous do?" To which David provided his own answer : "The Lord is in His holy temple, the Lord's throne is in heaven."

Mao Worship

Chairman Mao's throne is in Peking. His words take the place of Holy Writ. Lin Piao, Mao's heir apparent, in his Foreword to the 'Little Red Book' says : "Once Mao Tse-tung's thought is grasped by the masses, it becomes an inexhaustible source of strength and a spiritual atom bomb of infinite power." The martial music of the current national anthem *The East is Red* blares its message from every radio set many times a day :

> From the red east rises the sun,
> In China appears Mao Tse-tung,
> He works for the people's welfare,
> He is the people's great saviour.

The Communist Party is like the Sun,
Wherever it shines there is light,
Where the Communist Party goes,
There the people are liberated.

The cities were plastered with red paper inscribed with freshly written slogans far outdoing the traditional gaiety of the lunar New Year. China became a sea of red the year long. And day after day, above the noise of the traffic rose the tireless rhythm of the drums, the singing and the vociferous slogans 'Long live Chairman Mao!' as groups of Red Guards and young people paraded with the portraits of their hero-god and their banners. Michael Browne, a visiting Christian journalist, describes the deep fervour blazing in the young people's hearts for "our great leader, teacher, supreme commander and helmsman". The atmosphere, he said, was like that of a blazing old time revival—music, fervour, conversion testimonies, dedication, sacrifice. If only the object of adoration had been the Lord Jesus, China would be experiencing a mass movement of conversion!

A Christmas Surprise

On that bleak Christmas Eve 1967, a blind Christian and three of his friends were chatting in their Canton home. "Suddenly, above the din of drums and patriotic songs," he wrote in Braille to a friend, "over the radio we heard three Christmas carols from a Hong Kong station. Hearing these hymns our hearts were exceedingly happy : we were so overcome with joy we could not speak. The hymns were very, very soft and low but we still heard them very distinctly. I know that Jesus is always with me, so my heart is always happy and at peace"—the muted voice of China's 'Church in the shadows' is scarcely heard above the raucaus din of Mao worship.

The Confused Church

It is over twenty years since Communism came to power in China. For the Church, the initial ten years were traumatic. At first, unprepared and fearful, then flattered and bewildered by an unprecedented government patronage, the

Christian Church soon found itself in sad disarray in the face of the subtle tactics of the Communist government. Some church leaders used Holy Scripture to justify a policy of "be subject unto the higher power, for there is no power but of God : the powers that be are ordained of God". But others used Scripture to justify adopting the non-cooperative attitude of the persecuted Early Church : "We ought to obey God rather than man." Some went to prison and death for conscience sake. Others, with a clear conscience, accepted government jurisdiction and continued in a limited ministry in their churches. Men of all shades of theological convictions found themselves on both sides of the fence. Roman Catholics undoubtedly suffered more for their convictions than their Protestant fellow nationals.

The Fettered Church

By 1958, when the first Commune was instituted, the Christian Church was already a Church in fetters, though its leaders never ceased to protest their new found 'liberty'. Free from missionary control she certainly was, only to find herself firmly under state control. If Christians still professed to love the Church, they were required to place love for the country first: 'love country, love church' was the slogan. Where Christians had once rejoiced to 'Surrender hearts to Christ', now in 1958, they were urged to 'Hand over hearts to the Party !' Once they had insisted on the reality of things unseen. Now this world was all that mattered : social betterment was substituted for spiritual regeneration. Materialism took the place of idealism. Marxist realism pushed out Christian other-worldliness. Heaven now held greater promise than heaven hereafter. The powerful propaganda machine with great plausibility was incessantly putting the case for Communism. The children were given rosy pictures of it at school. Popular songs made it seem so attractive. The theatre, the cinema and the ballet eulogised heroes of the Revolution. The radio poured out hatred of imperialism, especially the U.S. variety, into every home. By 1959, TV stations were joining in the campaign in Peking, Shanghai, Canton and Hankow. Even railway journeys gave no relief from the martial music and the interminable propaganda speeches which blared on and on over every train's inter-com : from time to time teams of youthful persuaders moved down the coaches singing, dancing and praising Chairman Mao.

The Dwindling Church

The Christian Church survived, but only under severe restrictions. The number of congregations in the great cities was drastically reduced and few other towns were permitted more than one congregation. Redundant church buildings were turned to other uses. And inevitably this brought about some measure of union among the Protestant churches, as it was intended to do. But social and political activities arranged for Sundays made regular church attendance for the majority of Christians, especially the young, quite out of the question. As many as 80 per cent of the ordained ministers became redundant too and were sent to work in the factories or on the farms. In *Tien Feng*, the only Church magazine, the denunciation of certain Christian ministers by their fellow ministers as 'rightists' and 'reactionaries' drove some to suicide.

Despite the true situation, a party of six Australian churchmen who toured China in July 1959, the inaugural year of the Great Leap Forward, released a sympathetic report of what they were permitted to see and the half truths they were told by well-briefed church spokesmen. Other foreign visitors were similarly hoodwinked. Open opposition to the Three Self Patriotic Movement had ended and all branches of the Christian Church had been brought into line.

Readers of *Come Wind Come Weather* will know that the Protestant organisation sponsored by the Religious Affairs Bureau of the People's Government of China, was called the Three Self Patriotic Movement. 'Three self' indicates that this church was self-governing, self-supporting and self-propagating. Thus the familiar missionary objective for the Chinese Church was given a new twist. The slogan was now intended to mean the severance of all financial and administrative links with the missionary movement and with foreign 'imperialist' countries.

The Political Church

Y. T. Wu, the former YMCA General Secretary and chief figure in the Movement, wrote enthusiastically of the progress made by the Church during the first 'Great Decade' of Communist rule after breaking off the shackles of imperialism. At the Second National People's Congress in 1960 he spoke about the need for self-reform among Christians. The Christian press took its cue from the national press in contrasting the hell of the old regime with the heaven of the new society. And the vehement denunciation of missionaries as agents of imperialism continued.

Miss Gerde Buege, an East German, was able to revisit West China and to meet some of her old friends. She found Christians to be a frightening minority and was surprised that any church work survived at all amid the all-out attempts of the nation to catch up with the world economic standard through the Great Leap Forward campaign. She heard of pastors working in pickle factories, dairies and brickfields, or on the land; some of them, however, had been elected by the people as their local representatives. Mrs. Esther Nystrom, another former missionary, also paid a return visit to China in 1960 with a cultural group from Sweden; she attended Christian worship in each city visited, and called at the theological colleges in Peking and Nanking where Bishop K. H. Ting, a Vice-President of the Three Self Movement, was Principal. In the new China she observed no beggars, no prostitution, no alcoholism and no gangsterism. Mrs. Nystrom further discovered that a Commission set up in 1956 by the Three Self Patriotic Movement was working on a new translation of the Bible.

In January 1960, the Three Self Movement convened its second nation-wide conference in Shanghai. Three hundred and nineteen delegates from all parts of China attended and a new National Committee of one hundred and forty-five members was elected. Dr. Wu Yi-fang, a vice-chairman, reported that with the breakup of the 'counter-revolutionary ring' headed by Wang Ming-tao and Watchman Nee most reactionary forces had been cleared out of the Church. Though religious activities had been rearranged so as not to interfere with socialist production, Dr. Wu denounced as imperialist slander the suggestion that the Christian Church had suffered a severe blow as a result of the Great Leap Forward, Christians and the Chinese people breathed a common air. It was imperialism not the Church that had suffered a crushing blow. The tone of her speech made it clear that the conference was concerned not so much with how the churches could bear their witness in a Communist society as with their function as a political institution. Referring to the theological colleges, Dr Wu said that they had "carried through certain adjustments with increasing attention paid to politics". Regional conferences which followed all harped on the familiar 'anti-imperialism' theme and the dangers the church still faced from imperialist aggression.

Not long after this, the Peking Theological Seminary was closed and its students transferred to the Nanking Seminary, leaving a graduate research staff in Peking. The denigration of missionaries continued throughout 1961 with special emphasis on the way missionaries had used Sunday Schools to poison the children's minds with imperialism. Christians were sternly warned that missionary imperialism was still perpetrating sabotage against the New China. The following year the Board of Managers of the Nanking Union Seminary meeting to discuss theological education in China, emphasised the need for research into the imperialist use of religion.

The Remnant Church

Tien Feng's criticisms of certain country churches in Shantung and Chekiang suggest that they were maintaining a very lively witness. The following letter, written in 1961, describes church life in several northern provinces at that time :

"It is impossible to describe all that I have seen in a short letter. But God's work is still going on gloriously in the lives of many faithful Christians. We must give praise and thanks to God for His gracious care and protection. In the past the Church was built upon sand, and now it is being built on rock—the Rock. God does not make mistakes. I have been thankful to find brethren steadfast in their faith. This was seen particularly in many young people..."

In Shanghai, however, the China Bible Society was expelled from its premises, though it continued its work in the Moore Memorial Church. Sales and distribution of Scriptures were greatly reduced. Everyone felt the terrific pressure on time and strength in the achievement of material ends. But it was Christians who felt the pressure most; in a society which dismisses every spiritual value and frowns on all religious activity, the daily problem of how to maintain the spiritual life was acute. Girls labouring on farms found their only chance to pray was to rise at 3 a.m., while boys in college would miss breakfast so as to have a 'quiet time' or read their Bibles by night in the light of a street lamp.

Reports of a meeting of the Committee of the Three Self Movement held during August 1962 make it clear that the church was being drawn more and more into political activity in order to demonstrate its solidarity with the Chinese people. Church delegates sent abroad to various international conferences used the occasions to laud the Chinese government. Others, like Marcus Cheng and Francis Wei, were virulently denounced for criticising the government. Edgar Snow's book *Red China Today* (1962) often refers to the revolutionary hostility to religion in general, to the historic churches and to the missionary movement. After 1962, less and less specific information about the Chinese Church reached the world at large. But a Chinese reporter writing in the *Hong Kong Tiger Standard* of December 3rd, 1962, on the basis of information obtained from refugees, wrote of a decline in church attendance. As services had become so formal and so preoccupied with Marxist-Leninist propaganda, Christians, the article said, were meeting in private in small house groups, even at the risk of arrest for breaking the law forbidding private assembly. In 1958 a ban had been imposed on any meetings other than Sunday morning worship, including Sunday Schools, youth fellowships, women's meetings and Bible Study groups.

But the light of Christian witness was inextinguishable.

From Mao's own native Changsha came this letter, written in June 1962 :

"I am exceedingly glad to receive your letter. How good it is to remember one another though without communication for more than ten years. I trust that all is well with your work and with your family as well. We are separated physically, yet we never forget our fellowship in the Spirit. I have never ceased to do my church work throughout the past years. Premises in other places have also been as they were and services continue normally. I am now seventy-seven but still able to do all kinds of work . . . I know how to abound and how to be abased; everywhere and in all things I am instructed both to be full and to be hungry, both to abound and to suffer need. I truly thank God for being content in whatever state I am. Indeed, the barrel of meal wasted not, neither did the cruse of oil fail and in Christ all needs are fully met. May God's grace be upon you all !"

The Condemned Church

An article in *Tien Feng* in March 1963 was entitled 'Raise high the banners of anti-imperialism and patriotism and complete our present tasks !' Christians were lagging behind in political thinking, said the article, and the task of the Church was to develop Christian anti-imperialism through the study of socialism, strenuous efforts at self-reform and historical research. The next year the press launched a full-scale attack against all religion; church workers were accused of hiding their opposition to the government beneath a cloak of religion, of threatening peace and security, of lacking confidence in the government's policies and programmes, succumbing to the influences of imperialism and planning to increase the power of religion. "Religion is our enemy. Religion is guilty. Form a united front against religion." (*Red Flag*)

Miss Gerde Buege visited China again in 1965, but her itinerary was limited this time to Peking, Shanghai and Nanking, where she spent several days at the Theological Seminary. There she was interested to see the documentary "evidences of missionary involvement in imperialist aggression" exhibited in glass cases in the Library. There were eighty students, but so few could not begin to meet the needs for church workers in the future. She was told that outside the larger cities, church congregations were small. Foreign visitors were inevitably taken to the same church and met the same Christian spokesmen—usually Rev. Li Chu-wen of the Community Church in Shanghai and Secretary General of the Three Self Movement, Bishop K. H. Ting, President of the Nanking Union Theological Seminary and Vice-President of the Three Self Movement and Dr. Y. T. Wu, Chairman of the Three Self Movement. The comments of these men tended to disguise the fact that although it preserved its functions and ceremonies, the Church was barely tolerated, its activities were strictly limited and its membership was static. Whereas Rev. Li Chu-wen told a visiting Swedish Pentecostalist: "We are convinced that present conditions have brought us nearer to the centre of the Gospel, Evangelical Christianity in China will preserve its inner vitality and proclaim its message in a way that will meet man's spiritual needs", an Indian Christian attending the Ganefo and Chinese Sports Festival in Peking in September 1965 found a different impression. After worshipping at a poorly-attended church he said : "The Church in Communist China appears to have no future."

The Persecuted Church

In 1966, the blow fell. The full-scale offensive against religion was launched at last. With tremendous energy the Cultural Revolution attacked the 'old cultures'. All religions alike endured the desecration of their places of worship : temples, altars, mosques, shrines and churches. An orgy of destruction took place in Lhasa and the ancient Temple of Confucius in Shantung was seriously damaged. The situation became more serious for Christians than at any time since 1949. In August the South Roman Catholic Cathedral in Peking was seized and its religious symbols replaced with red flags, banners, busts or pictures of Mao and the inevitable red wall posters. The eight nuns of the Sacred Heart Convent were expelled from China, one of them dying as a result of her treatment, while all the statues of Christ and the Virgin were smashed. Roman Catholic and Protestant churches in Shanghai were shut down and Bibles, missals and prayer books burned in the streets. Again and again the Red Guards showed their vicious hatred for the Bible as they destroyed all they could find in fires at the church doors or in the public parks.

The story of Pastor Wong is one of many. He was serving a strong and faithful church when the Red Guards came to his town. Singling out the pastor and the church for attention as 'enemies of the people', they first rampaged recklessly through the church building and turned it into a shambles. Then they ordered the pastor and his wife to carry all the Bibles and hymn books into the street where they were compelled to kneel and burn them. They were then turned out of their home, and anyone attempting to help them was denounced as an 'enemy dog'. Mr. and Mrs. Wong eventually obtained jobs as labourers with barely sufficient wages to support them. Now forbidden to preach, Pastor Wong's life is a continuous sermon exalting Christ.

Violent attacks on the churches continued in April. Hardly a minister escaped. Canton, Swatow and Shanghai churches were purged by mid-summer. Nanking, Peking and other main cities followed. The Three Self Movement crumpled before the Red Guards. The purges were accompanied by fierce persecution of the Christians, many of whom were required to sit or kneel in the gutters to be mocked and spat upon. Others had their heads shaved to leave hair in the shape of a cross as a 'shameful identification'. Yet others were paraded through the streets as 'religious bad elements' to be ridiculed by the crowds. One minister working in a factory was made to wear a placard announcing "I am a liar and a deceiver", and forced to repeat the words at intervals before his jeering workmates. A woman church worker was brutally struck about the face. Another eighty year old Christian lady had her house ransacked and her Bible torn to pieces; ridiculing her for her faith, they tried to make her say "There is no God or Christ". "How could I," she replied, "after believing in Him for forty years?" Many pastors broke down and took their own lives.

One Christian couple in Shanghai were branded as capitalists—probably because of their pre-liberation university
training—ostracised and driven to take poison. In the
Peking reign of terror two Christian doctors took their own
lives.

Bishop K. H. Ting of Chekiang, a loyal supporter of the
Government, disappeared from public life in September.
Bishop Michael Chang of Fukien with both his suffragans
were placed in an indoctrination camp. Dr. James Ting, the
Methodist leader, after submitting to public humiliation was
also sent to the same camp.

Thus 1966 was the first year since the advent of Christianity to China that Christmas was not celebrated except
in the British Embassy in Peking and in the offices of the
British chargé d'affaires in Shanghai. Both buildings were
themselves to suffer during 1967 at the hands of rioting Red
Guards, and the chargé d'affaires in Shanghai (Mr. P. M.
Hewitt) was to be seriously injured by a mob.

Mr. and Mrs. Liu have six children. In 1961 Mrs. Liu
managed to leave China with the children, but Mr. Liu himself could not get a permit to leave. Mrs. Liu had paid
several previous visits to her husband, but when Mrs. Liu
last visited him the Red Guards had deprived him of his
comfortable apartment and he was living in a single room
where they had to speak in whispers lest they be overheard.
He had managed to keep his Bible hidden among the fire-
wood, but it was impossible for them to read or even to pray
aloud together. To get alone, the couple went for a walk in
the park, but it was so full of people that they could find no
place to pray—until the rain began to fall! Soon the park
was deserted and the Lius, though soaked, were alone! In
the downpour the two held hands and sang an old hymn
they had once memorized :

> Amid the trials that I meet,
> Amid the thorns that pierce my feet,
> One thought remains supremely sweet:
>   Thou thinkest, Lord, of me.

The Liquidated Church

By Easter 1967 the liquidation of the organised church in China was complete, as the following extracts indicate :

A Christian writing from Canton in November 1967 said :
"Now there is no God nor Buddha in Canton. Last year I occasionally attended some church services, but what I heard was something other than Christian messages. Now all churches in the city are closed. Church workers have been arrested, heads shaved smooth, paraded through the streets. Outside the churches are pasted big scrolls, above which is written 'Hang God!' Here no Scripture is to be heard; it is, of course, difficult to have the illumination of the Spirit. How I envy you people, can often read your Bible, gather together for meetings, hear the Word. My situation is discouraging indeed. Life is meaningless without any job to get a living. Circumstances keep me under bondage, making it impossible for me to taste the Lord's truth. Pray that the Lord may have mercy on me and hope that you can direct me to get on the way of the Cross."

Earlier, a mother of four wrote :
"The money you sent was duly received. Thanks to the faithful God who answered prayer, also to you for your love. God has not promised that the sky is always blue. Truly, the dark clouds may cover the earth for a while, but they soon disappear and the sky is clear again and the sun once more warms up our hearts. What a faithful and loving God indeed! How short is the period of a few months in life! Once more He let us experience afresh the lesson of faith and taste afresh the difficulties of life. Although there is no more any Big Book to read, yet how sweet it is when the Holy Spirit is with us Himself. Brother (her husband) came back once last year. It was an opportunity specially arranged by God Himself so that he could see his aged father once more. Thank God. We thought he would never come home again, how could one think that His almighty hand brought him home once more! He was dead, yet alive; lost, yet found. May two-

fold thanks be to Him. We live in the grace of God throughout. Never forget to pray for us, but do not write when it is not necessary."

Later she wrote :

"God is faithful and loving. He can sweep away the dark clouds so that light may shine upon us. But for the benefit of His children He often leaves over some Canaanites for us to keep practise fighting. This is a mystery of the spiritual world—the picture of our life. Being short of bread of life, we do at times feel distressed, even murmur like Habakkuk complaining 'Why?' However, with faith as shield, all these troubles vanish away. Around us, even within our family the attack of Satan is often felt. May God have mercy upon us. Please do not forget to pray for us. May the fellowship of the Holy Spirit be with us always."

But suffering sometimes has a purifying and refining influence. A Chinese pastor in Hong Kong received this letter from north China in 1968 :

"As I am an expert in engineering I held high post and received high salary. I quite enjoyed such life. But now as the result of the cultural revolution, I have lost my high post and my high salary and everything. I am now working just as a common labourer. However, I rejoice in gaining back the full joy in Christ. I know there are other friends who have the same experience."

The Hopeful Church

What of the future for religion in China? Members of a Japanese mission to Peking in mid 1967 were required to study Mao's *Quotations* at least five times a day. There were four Christians in the group and they confirmed that churches have all been closed for the time being. But Mrs. Anna Louisa Strong, the ageing authoress and long-time friend of Chairman Mao who lives in Peking, expressed to them the opinion that after the cultural revolution the doors of religious institutions will open again. Rev. Ian Thomson, who had once lived in China, spent three weeks in China in August 1967 but was given little freedom of movement. He met Red Guard propaganda on every train and plane and had to join in the study of Mao's *Quotations*. The churches he saw were all closed—some deserted, some used as schools. Mr. Thomson concludes his report with these words : "To sum it up, one cannot be in China today without being impressed by this happy, heaving mass of millions of Chinese, who, as no other people in the world today, I would guess, believe they know where they are going and are ecstatic about the prospect . . . Borne forward on the wings of belief in Mao and in their perpetual morning light they convey a feeling of strength and hope which one cannot but admire."

But Mr. Thomson had no contact with those who in this society are 'in the world but not of it'. For Christians the future must look less rosy, though they too are 'saved by hope'—the hope of better times, but ultimately the hope of Christ's Return. Meanwhile the survival of Christianity in China depends on the 'cell structure' church where Christians gather at regular times and in groups not larger than ten and often less than this. Such groups are known to be proliferating. And their witness is effective. "Tell us about Christianity," said a group of village people, "so that we may have the peace you have." "Tell us how to have joy like yours in the midst of such trials," said a teacher to a Christian girl in the Normal School. "I strongly suspect," writes one having contact with Christians in China, "that in terms of belief and practice, if not in outward and visible organisation . . . the Church is stronger than it was a decade ago . . ."

How can we help our Christian brethren in China? One obvious way is by broadcasting to China and letter extracts in the Appendix indicate the effectiveness of this means of communication. The disruption of central authority and laxity on the part of the police apparently makes it comparatively easy for Christians to listen to overseas broadcasts as well as to meet for fellowship. The Scriptures for instance are being read at dictation speed to enable Christians to replace their lost Bibles with portions of handwritten Scripture. For the time being, no other channels are open except that of intercession, the mighty power of which alone sustains this 'Church in the shadows' until the sun of a new day shines again.

CHAPTER III

BITTER LESSONS

THE Constitution of China, like that of the Soviet Union, contains a clause guaranteeing to her citizens freedom of religious belief. The Chinese Communists advertised this fact as they took over the country in 1949. Christians and those of other faiths were persuaded they had nothing to fear. Confirmation seemed to come in 1950 when a group of Church leaders was invited to Peking for three days as guests of the government—an honour without precedent even under a Christian head of state in the previous regime.*

Premier Chou En-lai explained that the People's Government had no quarrel with the Church as such. Its criticism was of the way in which the Church had been exploited by imperialist missionaries and the minds of Christians poisoned by imperialist thinking. If the Church wanted to enjoy its constitutional freedom, it must first "sweep the house clean" —meaning getting rid of the missionaries and their baneful influence—and accept the leadership of the Party. The Manifesto which embodied the acceptance of these demands placed the churches in a dilemma, but they found no alternative to requesting their missionary colleagues to withdraw.

As the missionaries departed, they left the churches bewildered and their leaders deeply divided. The official attitude was represented by the Manifesto and formed the policy of the newly founded Three Self Patriotic Movement. According to its terms, the Chinese Church would obey the Party and support the government in all its social and economic reforms in return for freedom to maintain and practise its own beliefs. Such a bargain appeared to be the only

*For the details of the events in the early part of this chapter, see *Come Wind, Come Weather* by Leslie Lyall (Hodder & Stoughton).

way to keep the Church in existence, and Scripture could be cited to defend this action. The great majority of leaders, therefore, adopted the official line.

But there were some like Mr. Watchman Nee and Mr. Wang Ming-tao who were not prepared to swallow the bait. Mr. Wang Ming-tao, pastor of the largest church in Peking and a man of nationwide influence, investigated the thinking described as 'imperialist poison', only to find that it included some of the essential and fundamental truths of the Christian faith and he said so publicly. His own church which he himself had founded had never known missionary control. While not uncritical of foreign missionaries on other grounds, he did not accept the thesis that they had been agents of imperialism. Many of the leaders in the Three Self Movement, on the other hand, were men whom he had often opposed on account of their liberal theology and of whose actions he now strongly disapproved. He therefore found it impossible to be unequally yoked with such men. Their policies, Mr. Wang believed on the authority of Scripture, were doomed to eventual failure. Thus he refused to throw in his lot with the Three Self Movement and took a resolute stand against the cooperation with the government which most of the country's church leaders had accepted.

Who was right? Mr. Wang Ming-Tao went to prison in 1955 to serve a life sentence for his adherence to principle, and his church was disbanded. (After twelve years in a Peking gaol, the sixty-eight year old pastor was moved to a labour camp in Tatung, North Shansi in 1968.) Many of those who shared Mr. Wang's view also went to prison. The Three Self Movement churches, on the other hand, continued to function for a further ten years, though greatly reduced in number. Patriotism became their chief concern and to promote this among Christians the Government provided funds for the indoctrination of the clergy. Sermons became increasingly political in tone, while doctrines like the end of the age and the Coming of Christ were taboo. In such an atmosphere, many Christians became disillusioned and began to enjoy true fellowship in small unpublicised house meetings. It was left to the Cultural Revolution to tear the mask off the face of Communism and to reveal it as the bitter foe of religion : all churches were closed regardless of their nature and even the most slavish supporters of the Government, such as Bishop K. H. Ting, found themselves, to their chagrin, in prison or in labour camps.

This tragic story of men who suffered, some for their opposition to the Three Self Movement and some in spite of their faithful adherence to the Party line and leadership in the Three Self Movement, demands careful examination. It has important lessons for the rest of the world. What really was the Three Self Patriotic Movement? Was it a genuine Christian Church or a distortion of true Christianity? Was it a spontaneous expression of Christian convictions or a Communist imposed strait-jacket? Were the leaders free agents or stooges? What did it accomplish in the ten borrowed years following the imprisonment of Watchman Nee and Wang Ming-tao?

From the first, the opinions of foreign observers differed. The Anglican quarterly, *East West Review* (Jan. 1960), expressed the view that the developments in the Chinese Church were the result of genuine Christian convictions and not Communist pressures. Church leaders, said the writer, were emphatically not stooges. On the other hand, a former China missionary, applying the historic tests of a true church—the *faithful* preaching of the Word of God and the *true* observance of the sacraments—concluded that the Three Self Church, being an essence of Christianity diluted in order to conform to state demands, could no longer be regarded as a Christian Church. These opinions represent two opposing viewpoints. It is admittedly difficult for those outside China to 'judge righteous judgment' as the Apostle Paul would have us do. But in the interests of truth we must balance sympathy for fellow Christians in an exceedingly difficult situation with an assessment of what are the facts, as far as we can know them.

The Three Self Movement made great claims for itself. To celebrate, a *Tien Feng* article in the October 10th, 1959 issue, 'Ten Years of Struggle in opposing Imperialism and Loving our Country', described the Church before 1947 as a tool of the missionaries for their private and imperialistic purposes and proceeded to outline the Church's achievements since then : while missionaries had opposed the Manifesto in 1950, four hundred thousand Christians had welcomed it; in the nationwide Denunciation Movement in 1951 the manipulation of religion by imperialism had been exposed; in 1953 Wang Ming-tao, Watchman Nee and their counter-revolutionary organisation had attempted to destroy the Three Self Movement, but their mad opposition had finally been overcome in 1955; the Rectification Campaign of 1956–7 had further exposed the Rightists in the Church and the 'semi-colonial' denominations had begun to work together; the Socialist Education Movement had proved effective in remoulding the thinking of Christians and preparing them for the Great Leap Forward the following year. Thus, in ten years, the Three Self Movement, 'under the guidance of the Party', had grown to maturity and a fundamental change in the aspect of the Church had taken place : alien imperialism in the churches had been curbed, rightist elements had been eliminated, the Three Self programme for full autonomy carried out and a solidarity with the whole Chinese people in their march toward socialism achieved. Parades of Christians took place in many cities as part of the celebrations at the end of 'the Great Decade'. Over and over again the Church spokesmen protested their new-found freedom from imperialist domination under the sympathetic leadership of the Party. They repeated such phrases as 'naked imperialist aggression', the 'imperialist use of missionary work' and 'the poison of imperialist thinking' in reference to the whole missionary movement. Missionaries were described as 'Bible-reading wolves'. The Boxer massacre of Christians and foreign missionaries in 1900 was justified as an inevitable struggle against the imperialists who had been 'perpetrating abusive and criminal activities throughout the greater part of China'. In 1960 Y. T. Wu, the General Secretary of the Movement, confessed the continuing need for self-reform among Christians and for eternal vigilance against the perpetual dangers to the Church from imperialist aggression. Two years later, *Tien Feng* was still complaining that

Christians lagged behind in political thinking and needed to develop 'Christian anti-imperialism'.

How far were the Church leaders really speaking for themselves, or to what extent were they ventriloquist dolls? If they were speaking for themselves, they had nothing to say about the Church's obligation to proclaim the Gospel of Christ throughout their country, little to say that was positively Christian, a lot to say about the crimes of the missionaries and a very great deal to say about socialism. Their speaking and writing are evidence of the remarkable success of the indoctrination programme. But were they in fact speaking with their own voices?

One defector from China to the free world was Mr. Edward C. M. Chen, who for ten years had been an official of the Religious Affairs Bureau, a government department which deals with all religious bodies and appoints separate officials and committees for each religion. Comrade Chen was a young cadre who, because of his political reliability, was at an early stage given sole responsibility for managing religious affairs in Canton. His ten years in 'religious front work' gave him ample opportunity to gain a unique understanding of the relationship of the Chinese Communist Party to the Christian Church. In his written statements Mr. Chen insists that the basic dispute between Christians and Communists is not political but philosophical and social. Consequently the struggle against the Christian target is not one to be carried out openly and formally, but takes on the character of 'an invisible battle'. Thus the official policy was not to seek outright extermination but restriction, reformation and utilisation with total control as the end in view. Confronted with this policy, said Mr Chen, religious organisations were "travelling down a difficult and abnormal road and were gradually withering away."

With this goal clearly in view, the Three Self Reform Movement was set up. Only those 'with political awareness' were permitted to serve on the 'preparation committees' in 1950. Resistance on the part of Roman Catholics and some Protestant bodies to the use of the word 'reform' led to the substitution of 'patriotic' in the title. The Three Self Patriotic Movement was to cooperate with the Religious

United Front. Official directives distinguished between Roman Catholics and Protestants (easier to control!), and, among Protestants, between the 'social Gospel' group (enlightened!) and the 'spiritual' group (conservative, obstinate, opposed to the Three Self Movement!). Comrade Chen knew nothing about religion initially, but was instructed to study religious organisations, investigate their leaders, control all kinds of activity, bring Catholics and Protestants into the Three Self Movement, keep religious leaders informed about government policies and so raise their political awareness, push believers into socialist action, search out hidden reactionaries, entertain foreign religious guests and reduce the influence of religion. As regards 'freedom of religious belief', Comrade Chen was instructed that this meant that all religious activity had to be strictly confined to official buildings so as not to interfere with the beliefs of others and for the same reason all activities out-of-doors and in private homes were prohibited. In the name of religious freedom, religious workers were not allowed to exercise any form of discipline or social influence over their followers, a restriction which led to frequent clashes and controversies. Chen describes methods used to infiltrate the churches either by using individuals as spies or by openly interpreting passages of Scripture from a Marxist point of view. It was the declared aim of the government to win over as many preachers and evangelists as possible to the side of the government by a reinterpretation of the Bible in Marxist terms. To this end enormous sums of money were made available to the committee of the Three Self Movement for the purpose of indoctrinating the leaders and making religion serve politics.

This revealing document makes it clear that even Miss Helen Willis in her fascinating book *Through Encouragement of the Scriptures* was mistaken in saying that "This Movement was planned by and is under the control of the modernist pro-government intellectuals in the Church." They neither planned it nor did they control it. The Movement was a Communist government creation and controlled from beginning to end by the government through the officials of the Religious Affairs Bureau. The Three Self

Patriotic Movement was quite evidently not the spontaneous creation of the churches themselves. Were the Three Self leaders too blind to recognise this or were they completely taken in by the clever blandishments and subtle methods of the Communists or were they intimidated? They were clearly stooges, but did they become such consciously or unconsciously, willingly or unwillingly?

Mr. Wang Ming-tao despite his intense suffering, was at least spared the humiliation of witnessing the final disillusionment and failure of fifteen years' efforts to preserve a church's existence by dubious compromises.

The bitter lessons of this chapter in church history are two. The first is that it is always right to stand firm on Biblical principles, whatever the personal cost, while it is never right for Christians to allow mere expediency to determine their actions. Surely God was honoured more by Mr. Wang's courageous stand and the imprisonment of Mr. Nee and hundreds of others than by the adoption of what seemed expedient if the churches were to continue to function.

The other lesson is the futility of believing Communist protestations and propaganda about religious freedom. The Communist interpretation of 'freedom of religious belief' is that "those who believe in religion have freedom and those who are opposed to it have their religious freedom too". "You have freedom to believe what you like and we have freedom to oppose your beliefs," they say. Acting on this principle, special coures of indoctrination for pastors were arranged, designed to shake their Christian convictions. Now if freedom of religious beliefs is not also freedom to preserve that belief against all opposition and to proclaim it openly it has little meaning. But it is an unchangeable Communist principle that 'religious activities must return to the churches'; in other words the public must at all costs be protected from any kind of Christian 'proselytism'. In China and, for twenty years in Europe, this has been consistent Communist policy.

It has long been clear to the world, and the more so since the Cultural Revolution, that freedom of religious belief in orthodox Communist countries is not what we in the West understand by freedom. In China it was a piece of window-dressing to impress other Asian nations but was never intended to permit the exercise of full religious freedom. Where in the whole Communist world has there been any genuine intellectual or religious freedom? But the night may be passing. In Europe, notably in Czechoslovakia, the people, including Christians have had a brief taste of freedom from Stalinist tyranny. Eventually, even Russian tanks will fail to stem the rising tide against despotism. In China, too, the fury of the Cultural Revolution has failed to uproot those who insist on a more human brand of socialism; 'revisionists' or 'liberalisers' are still strong. Perhaps, not only in Czechoslovakia but in other Communist countries, including China, the day of greater freedom may be closer than we think. Red sky at night holds the promise of fair weather tomorrow.

CHAPTER IV

BRIEF GUIDE TO COMMUNISM

IT is of the first importance that everyone should know, quite clearly and objectively what Communism or Marxism is all about. It is far easier to be swayed emotionally by stories of Communist atrocities and suffering under Communism rather than to reach an objective assessment of this powerful system. However true such stories may be, they scarcely help us to understand what the Communist philosophy is and why Communists behave in the way they do. Nor do sensational stories explain why so many millions in the world today pin their future hopes for a better life on the promises of Communism. We therefore offer a brief encyclopaedia of Communism in order to whet the appetite for more extensive reading in the vast literature on the subject.

Karl MARX (1818–83) was a German Jew and came from a long line of rabbis whose intellect he inherited. His father took the family away from the synagogue to join the Lutheran Church. In his teens, Karl, a very thoughtful lad, wrote a pamphlet on communion with God. At Bonn University he spent a stormy year, gave up his belief in God and earned his father's disapproval as an egotist. At Berlin University he adapted the dialectical thesis of Professor Georg Hegel to his own purpose, substituting 'matter' for 'idea'. Thus, when thesis fights antithesis, the conflict results in the discovery of a new synthesis and this, according to Marx, is the law of man's social progress. After gaining his Ph.D. Marx moved to Cologne and then Paris where he married a boyhood friend. In Paris he was introduced to Friedrich Engels, his life-long friend and collaborator. There too he studied economics and reached the historic conclusion that economics is the sole power behind society's dialectical progress.

This law, which he called economic determinism or scientific socialism, held for him the vision of inevitable progress towards the final perfect human society. When he was expelled from France he moved to Brussels where the *Communist Manifesto* was published and the first Communist Party formed in 1848. Moving to London, Marx lived there for the rest of his life. Domestically, it was a tragic life, but in London he wrote and published his masterpiece *Capital*.

Vladimir LENIN (1870–1924), a Russian, was the man who translated Marx's theories into practice and, thirty-four years after Marx's death, achieved the first successful revolution — the October Revolution of 1917. Lenin had lived in exile from Russia since 1900. He and Trotsky held different convictions about Party discipline and the use of violence in revolution and had finally parted company in 1912. Then, in 1917, as Russia faced defeat at the hands of Germany, Lenin returned to Russia where Trotsky was already trying to achieve his kind of revolution and became the first President of a new republic, with Trotsky as Foreign Secretary. From 1918 to 1921 civil war raged throughout Russia with the Communists having to resist the interference of foreign troops trying to support the Czar. In 1922 Lenin founded the U.S.S.R. His contribution to Communist doctrine lay in his analysis of imperialism as the last stage of capitalism before the victory of socialism and the revolutionary prospects arising out of this situation. He died in 1924 as a result of injuries received in an attempted assassination.

Joseph STALIN (1879–1953) was exiled six times before the 1917 Revolution. He too was an egotist and carried on the work of Lenin. He instituted the first Five Year Plan, carried out the Agrarian Revolution of 1929–33 and introduced collective farming methods. Abroad, he directed, unsuccessfully, the new Communist Party in China from its foundation in 1921. The successful defence of Russia against Nazi Germany and the victories of Leningrad and Stalingrad gave him great prestige which facilitated the post-war territorial expansion of Russia and the securing of a protective ring of satellite Communist states including East Germany and Berlin. 'Stalinism' has become the name for brutal suppression of freedom of expression. Tens of thousands were sent without trial to Siberia or sentenced to death by the orders of Stalin whose inordinate pride encouraged a personality cult of himself. He is still a hero in China.

Nikita KHRUSCHEV (1894–   ) was the man who in 1956 denounced Stalin, exposed his crimes, succeeded to power and introduced 'destalinisation' policies. For these he earned the hatred of the Chinese. He made a vigorous attack on the Christian Church in Russia. Eventually he was forced out of power in 1964.

MAO Tse-tung (1893–   ) is a native of Hunan, China. In 1911 he witnessed the Nationalist Revolution in Changsha from a hilltop and dedicated his life to revolution. After five years of a good education, he became Assistant Librarian in Peking University where he acquired an interest in Marxism, and while editing student magazines in Hunan he became a convinced Marxist. The Chinese Communist Party was formed in 1921 and soon Mao was authorised to organise the peasants of his native province. He supported the Northern March to the River Yangtze in 1926–7 and was in Changsha when the Communists broke with Chiang Kaishek and the Nationalists. He led the Autumn Uprising in Hunan, but his lack of success brought criticism on his head. In 1931 he engaged in a bloody and ruthless rise to power and began to propound his guerilla warfare theories which were based on the tactics of Sun Tzu (500 B.C.). He lost some of his authority during the Kuomintang encirclement in Kiangsi, but was one of the heroes of the Long March from Kiangsi in South China to Yenan, Shensi, in North China in 1934–5. The following year he gained control of the Communist Party machine and approved of the kidnapping of Chiang Kai-shek at the end of that year. The outcome was an agreement to form an anti-Japanese coalition with the Kuomintang which led to the outbreak of the Sino-Japanese war in September 1937. Mao's greatest literary output took place in the years 1938–40 when also his guerilla warfare theories were successfully put to the test against the Japanese army. During the years 1942–44 Mao achieved the

Sinification of Marxist theory and practice by one of the first 'rectification' campaigns and so established Chinese independence from Moscow. At the seventh Congress of the Chinese Communist Party in 1945 the *Thoughts of Mao* were declared to be the official guide for the Party in the post-war years and the cult of Mao began to blossom. Meanwhile Mao Tse-tung and Stalin reached an agreement as to their mutual policies and, when the Japanese army surrendered, the Communist armies found themselves in a strategic position to accept that surrender, while the Nationalist forces in West China were remote from the scene. Mao now met President Chiang Kai-shek in Chungking to negotiate about the future, but the failure of these talks led to a resumption of civil war in which the smaller but better organised and more dedicated Communist forces gained the victory over numerically superior forces with poor morale and incompetent leadership. Following the total occupation of China and the withdrawal of the Nationalist Government to Formosa, the Communists held the first meeting of the People's Political Consultative Council in September 1949. On October 1st Chairman Mao Tse-tung proclaimed the foundation of the Chinese People's Republic from the Tien An Gate of the Forbidden City in Peking. In December of the same year, Mao met Stalin for the first time to conclude a Treaty of Friendship. When Stalin died in 1953 Mao assumed his mantle and was bitterly critical of Khruschev's 'destalinisation' policies. In particular Mao was vehemently opposed to Russia's declared willingness to forgo force as a tool of revolution in favour of 'peaceful coexistence' with the capitalist world. The deliberate use of violence to achieve the Communist goal is an essential Marxist dogma to which China tenaciously clings. Mao's famous dictum deserves quoting in full : "Political power grows out of the barrel of a gun. Violent revolution is a universal law of proletarian revolution. The seizure of power by armed force, the settlement of issues by war is the central task and the highest form of revolution. Only with guns can the whole world be transformed." Thus China continues to admire the discredited Stalin whose mantle Mao proudly assumed. Consequently, friction developed between China and the

U.S.S.R. in which Khruschev was the irritating factor. In 1958 Mao announced the organisation of the Communes and the Great Leap Forward programme. Two years later China admitted the failure of the plan. In 1960 the U.S.S.R. and the satellite nations of East Europe denounced China. A diplomatic breach between China and Russia led to the withdrawal of all Russian advisors and technicians. 1960 and 1961 were bitter years of famine and attempts to compensate for the crippling loss of Soviet technical aid. In 1963 the diplomatic break with Russia became complete. To bolster his own waning authority, Mao planned the Great Proletarian Cultural Revolution in 1965 and in the following year unleashed the revolutionary energies of China's youth in the Red Guard movement. The years 1967 and 1968 were years of confusion as China broke up into multiple rival factions struggling for power and fighting among themselves. Although all pay lip service to Mao, a powerful anti-Mao sentiment exists. Rejecting his extremist supporters and turning to the Army, Mao formed new 'three way alliances' which in turn established 'revolutionary committees' to replace the old Party machinery.

Materialism in Communist terms, is not the love of material things or worldliness, but the philosophy which declares that "the material world to which we belong is the only reality" (Marx). Matter is eternal and mind is the highest expression of matter, not something distinct from it. The universe can only be analysed and understood through scientific observation. Thus Communism rules out the existence of God and the supernatural, and so naturally denies the deity of Christ. It excludes any possibility of the existence of a soul in man or life after death and a future judgment. It denies the existence of any eternally valid moral law. Atheism is thus basic to Communist dogma which substitutes its own comprehensive view of the universe, man, life, death, society, economics, religion, ethics and culture.

Dialectical Materialism is the central tenet of Communism and, as the supposed scientific explanation of history, provides a Communist substitute for the Sovereign Creator and

Ruler of mankind and the universe. Dialectical Material-ism presupposes a material universe in which there is no place for the supernatural. Marx accepted the original theory propounded by the German philosopher Georg Hegel (1770–1831) of Berlin University who explained the natural development of ideas as a kind of debate or argument (cf. Gk. 'dialektos') a general proposition or thesis is contested and gives rise to a 'contradiction' or antithesis. Further de-bate reconciles these opposites in a synthesis which at once becomes a new thesis and the process then repeats itself. Marx made the theory the clue to the inner meaning of his-tory and his own original contribution was the 'discovery' that economics was the force which causes this law of motion to operate. The basic fact of existence being man's need to eat in order to live, all life centres around the pro-duction of food or of those commodities which can be ex-changed for food. Marx went on to demonstrate that his-tory has always evolved in a series of revolutions resulting from conflicts and tensions between two classes – those who own the means of production and those who operate them but do not own them. This "matter arguing with itself causes historical progress" (de Koster). Or, to put it graph-ically, social progress proceeds in a forward and upward direction, but, instead of moving in a straight line, its path-way is a series of predestined zig-zags. Such is the rhythm of history. The end of the process will be the classless society when the state will wither away and man will at last live under Utopian conditions. This law of motion, sometimes referred to as scientific socialism, is considered to be as in-violable as the laws of physics or astronomy. By understand-ing this built-in law of history, we can not only interpret the whole of past history but also predict with perfect accuracy the future course of history. But for Marx philosophy was merely a guide to action. By making his actions conform with this law, man can hasten the attainment of the perfectly just human society.

History of Society. The Marxist sees this as a dialectical pro-gression from a primitive tribal society (communistic) to a slave society, from a slave society to feudalism, from feudal-

ism to capitalism, from capitalism to socialism and ultimately from socialism to communism. This progress was
determined by economic factors – by developing means of
production and the struggle for their control. Man rose from
the ape stage by his tool-making activities. Progress was
then determined by the developing sophistication of the
tools used in production and the struggle to own and control
those tools. Man's labours thus created our world. This
philosophy of history based on Dialectical Materialism is
called Historical Materialism. The current crisis facing
capitalism, and the worldwide growth of socialism encourage
Communists in their confidence in the reliability of their
prophecies.

Class Struggle. Classes are sections of people who earn their
living in the same way. In Marx's day, there were basically
two classes; those who owned the tools or the machinery of
production but who did not work them (the capitalists) and
those who worked them but did not own them (the workers
or proletariat). In the present day, the two-class idea is not
so easily justified. The emergence of private ownership first
led to class struggles. Subsequent history has consisted of
class struggles, and the culmination of the class struggle of
war will be the violent overthrow of the capitalist system so
that the working class can become the ruling class and build
a socialist society – 'the dictatorship of the proletariat'. Both
Marx and Lenin always insisted on the necessity for revolution to be violent. The culmination will be a classless society
and the end of the dialectical process. Then real history will
begin! The tension between classes generates the dynamic
which results in further progress. The same is true of 'contra-
dictions' within Communism, disputes over policy and conflicts between the conservatives and the progressives within
a country. It is essential to keep 'struggle' alive if progress is
to be maintained.

Socialism. The structure of society after the downfall of
capitalism as a result of revolution is called socialism; it
involves the total nationalisation of all means of production
and planned production on a national scale. At this stage the
principle of reward for labour is "from each according to

his ability, to each according to his work". Clearly the incentive motive still prevails under socialism, in its first stage.
But as production soars and there is abundance for all, a new
principle is introduced "From each according to his ability, to each according to his need." This is the stage at which
full 'communism' is reached. The incentive motive will
have gone. The world is at present still in the socialist stage,
but moving towards the goal of 'communism'. China, with
her communes, has tried to hasten the progress but Mao has
denounced 'economism' which involves the incentive motive
as a backward step in the direction of capitalism – 'following
the capitalist road'.

Capital (or *Das Kapital*) is the Karl Marx masterpiece and
the Bible of Communism. It was printed in three volumes
in 1867, 1885 and 1894 (posthumously). In this work Marx
reaffirms the contents of the *Communist Manifesto* (1848)
and uses economic arguments to prove that capitalism must
inevitably enrich the few and impoverish the majority. The
main thesis is that concerning 'surplus value' which asserts
that the value of any commodity consists solely in the
human labour time involved in its production. "Value is
found only in labour." In order to make a profit—the reason
for owning a factory—the owner (capitalist) pays the
workers less than the value of their labours, the surplus from
sales thus representing his profits. As increased mechanisation takes place, less human labour is employed and so
profits decrease. To compensate himself the owner must
further exploit his remaining labour force. Circumstances
will force capitalists to indulge in 'take-overs' and to combine so that capital will become concentrated in the hands of
fewer and fewer monopolists. Thus the worker is driven by
the operation of the labour market to the bare level of subsistence and the owners enrich themselves at the expense of
the workers. The antagonised workers (or proletariat) engage in a kind of perpetual warfare of struggle against the
owners (or bourgeoisie) until the moment is reached when
they rise up and overthrow the capitalists in a violent revolution. Then they set up the dictatorship of the proletariat
which in turn prepares the way for the final abolition of

classes and the classless society. Marx makes the mistake in his book of generalising from isolated case histories and of substituting subjective myths for objective truths. Although some of the theories and prophecies in the book are demonstrably mistaken, nevertheless this is one of the most influential books ever written.

Ethics. As man is purely a social product, the Marxist sees culture, morality, philosophy and religion as "the product of the economic stage which society has reached at any particular epoch". The forms of economic production determine social existence. This is 'economic determinism'. "We therefore reject every attempt to impose on us any moral dogma whatsoever as an eternal, ultimate and for ever immutable law" (*The Manifesto*). Man is the product of economic forces. What he believes, thinks and likes, his religious ideas, philosophy and ethics are all the outcome of the current economic era. Thus, all moral values are only relative, having grown out of material conditions and are in a constant state of flux. There are no permanent and unchanging principles of conduct. Man has no ultimate accountability for his conduct. "Class interest is the mother of ethics." Evil is thus not in man but in the faulty economic system. So man individually needs no redemption. Religion being the product of economics, is merely another reflection of the class struggle. During the revolutionary period, the one ethical principle is the consideration 'Does my action serve the class struggle? Does it further the cause of Communism? If it does, it is right. If it does not, it is a crime against the people.' "Our morality is wholly subordinated to the interests of the class struggle" (Lenin). The end always justifies the means. This explains the use of violence and cruelty during the fight to gain power. Once power is gained their use usually diminishes. It also explains the ruthlessness in removing every obstacle in the way of progress towards Communism. At the same time Communists are urged to overcome the selfishness of a class society, to lead an exemplary life, to work hard and to devote themselves to the common good.

·   ·   ·

In opposing Communism, Christians should know what it is to which they are opposed. They should be quite clear, for instance, that Christianity is not allied to capitalism or to any kind of social or economic theory. Christianity is not therefore necessarily opposed to the social experiments of Communism, which have much to commend them, especially in under-developed countries. China's own achievements in this sphere are remarkable. Economically, too, Communism has in some respects been very successful in Russia and in China, though some western economists might disagree with its economic theories and be quick to point out their fallacies. But in these two spheres where the West has yet to put its own house in order, the Christian is not called upon to pass judgment. In any case, Christians who actually live in countries with Communist governments are obliged to accept the existing social arrangements and to live loyally under the prevalent economic system, just as in our western democracies the nation as a whole must accept the policies of the party in power, however much individuals may disagree with those policies. The Christian is never called to become a revolutionary in a political sense, but to be the salt of the society in which he lives. No! Christianity is in conflict with Communism mainly on account of its incompatible basic philosophy. The Christian rejects Communism as a way of life on ideological or theological grounds. He cannot accept its atheism and materialism nor the false theories which are based upon them. Communism's denial of the unique claims of the Lord Jesus Christ would force the Christian to oppose it on this ground alone. Moreover, the ruthlessness and the hatred, the inevitable tyranny and the limitation of personal freedom which are essential ingredients of orthodox Communist practice are to the Christian utterly abhorrent.

A Christian, therefore, in order to combat Communism must know what his own beliefs are and equally must have a clear understanding of the beliefs and practices of his Communist neighbours or work-mates. The foregoing brief summary of orthodox Communist belief may serve as an introduction to this important study.

CHAPTER V

A DECEPTIVE COUNTERFEIT

THERE are, around the world, naïve people who, recognising the good features in both Christianity and Communism, still ask the question :

"Can you be a Christian and a Communist?"

To which the reply must be :

"Impossible ! You might as well ask 'Can you be black and white at the same time?' "

"But the late Dean of Canterbury was both, wasn't he?"

"With respect, the Dean was a deluded man and a too willing tool of his Chinese Communist acquaintances."

"But there have been others who claim that Communism is the real Christianity with its passion for social justice and the rights of man and its intense longing for the perfect social order, for permanent peace and a world in which we may enjoy the fulness of life. Already, they claim, Communist countries have higher moral standards than Christian countries : they have done away with organised vice, gambling and divorce—things which so disgrace most western nations. What do you say to that?"

"I agree that Communism in its early stages does have a puritanical spirit in relation to public morals and that what you say is to a large extent true still of China. Things seem to be slipping in other Communist countries. I am aware that they despise our 'degenerate bourgeois morals'. But it is a mistake merely to equate Christianity with certain codes of ethics or with a particular kind of social order. While there are clearly social and moral applications of Christian truth which are of the highest importance, Christianity's primary concern is not with the social order or with social reform."

"What then is Christianity's primary concern?"

"With God—the living God, revealed in Jesus Christ—and man's relation to God. And, of course, Communism is concerned with the denial of God's existence and consequently the spiritual nature of man. In place of this, Communism has a philosophy of materialism which totally rules out the supernatural—God, spirit, soul, life after death, heaven and hell."

"So Christianity and Communism are quite incompatible and irreconcilable?"

"Yes, exactly. And the Communists themselves are the first to insist on this. Go back to the prophets of Communism. Karl Marx declared that 'the material world to which we belong is the only reality'. To the argument that mind is distinct from matter, Marx replies, 'No. Mind is merely the highest product of matter', thereby denying the possibility of a Supreme Mind which created and now directs the world. It follows that there is no God. Friedrich Engels, Marx's closest friend and collaborator, expressed his view when he said 'All religion is unspeakable baseness!' Douglas Hyde, an ex-Communist and one-time news editor of the *Daily Worker*, has said 'Communism does not simply say "There is no God". It goes on to say 'Men everywhere must be made to cease believing in Him!' 'Religion,' argued Marx, 'is the opium of the people' because, like opium, it dulls the senses to present pain and intolerable social evils and conjures up a non-existent dream world of heaven-to-come. Thus it is a positive hindrance to social change because it makes people acquiesce in the status quo."

"So you don't think it possible to be both a Communist and a Christian?"

"Surely, this is obvious. The two philosophies are mutually antagonistic. They cancel out one another. Dr. Fred Schwartz says, 'Communism without atheism is cancer without malignancy, a contradiction in terms." Either the one or the other is true. They can't both be true. The Christian can find no place in his thinking for the militant atheism of Marx and Mao, and Communism can find no place in its materialism for idealism—the supremacy of ideas—or the conception of a Supreme Mind, the truth of God the Creator. Even to contemplate the possibility of becoming a practising Communist while remaining a convinced Christian requires either the most utter self-deception or the most abysmal ignorance both of Christianity and of Communism."

.   .   .

When the Red Guards displayed their poster in Shanghai
with the slogan 'Hang God!' they were in fact openly declaring what Chinese Communists, as orthodox Marxists,
had always believed—that all religion is supersitition and
in the interests of truth must be destroyed. Their earlier
tolerant pose toward the Christian churches in China was a
subtle tactic designed to achieve the purpose of final destruction. The Three Self Patriotic Movement was a
Haman's gallows on which to hang, not only God, but the
Christian Church in China. It was a Communist plot to
enslave the Church, to undermine the faith of Christians
and to prevent the effective witness of the Church in
Chinese society. The moment of truth arrived when the
Cultural Revolution finally closed the church doors and put
the Three Self leaders in prison or labour camps. Even if the
movement were ever to be revived, as a temporary expedient,
no one can ever again be in doubt about the ultimate purpose of Chinese Communism. Religion and superstition
have never been out of the headlines in China. The vigorous campaign against both has been conducted by a number
of very able writers.

There were other purposes in creating the Three Self
Patriotic Movement—it was intended to express hatred for
foreign missions by severing all relations with them; it was
further designed to promote patriotism above every other
loyalty, whether family or religious; and it was also created
in order to lull the rest of Asia into a false security on religious ground.

Asian lands suffer generally from weak and corrupt
government and the people consequently cannot achieve
the standard of living they deserve. Does China's example
of economic progress hold out the hope that Communism
could be the answer to their problems? Asian countries
would certainly welcome the economic and social benefits
China has begun to enjoy. But Hindus, Buddhists and

Muslims are alike suspicious of the well-known atheism of
Communism. Would they have to swallow this pill as the
price of progress? This is precisely the problem, the chief
barrier to the export of Chinese Communism. At the Afro-
Asian Conference at Dandung in 1955, the delegates re-
affirmed one of the basic principles for the future peaceful
cooperation between nations taken from Indonesia's *Pantja
Sila* or Five Principles, namely 'Faith in one God'. So
Chinese Communist leaders set out to persuade Asia that
Communism is tolerant toward all religions. Her propaganda incessantly tells Muslims everywhere that Chinese
Muslims are free and their mosques unmolested. In May
1961 they publicised the state visit of a Buddhist delegation to China, which came to escort a sacred relic on a visit
to Ceylon : on its return to China it would be housed in a
new pagoda. In such ways Communists deceive Muslims
and Buddhists into thinking that their fellow religionists
in China enjoy full freedom. And Christian churches in
Peking, Shanghai and Nanking once served the same purpose — to delude visitors into believing that religious freedom
for Christians exists in China. The propaganda to this effect
enticed thousands of Chinese Christians back to China from
Indonesia in 1960 when there were difficulties there for
Chinese. They regretted their decision to return almost as
soon as they arrived in China. One boy wrote "I have just
arrived, but there is no place here to worship and moreover, it is not possible to do so. My spiritual life is now very
weak . . . pray that we may return to a place where there
is a church." Premier Chou En-lai on his official foreign
tours frequently visits temples and mosques, so creating the
impression that Communists respect religion and cannot be so
anti-religious after all. Carefully chosen and reliable Christian leaders have been sent to European and Asian countries
all on similar missions. This deliberate playing down for
foreign consumption of Communist atheist and anti-religious
policies is just a part of the great conspiracy, a tactic in the
battle for world conquest, the big lie that is really believed.

. . .

"Would you say that events have confirmed the worst fears

of Chinese Christians and vindicated the firm stand of men like Mr. Wang Ming-tao?"

"Undoubtedly. They have also made the many advances from foreign individuals and groups of many denominations and nationalities and shades of political colour look, at best, naïve and at worst, ridiculous. By the very nature of things nothing could be gained by any dialogue between members of a Communist created and Communist directed religious organisation such as the Three Self Patriotic Movement in China and individuals or groups from other lands representing completely free churches and organisations.

"It seems tragic that the Chinese and Russian Communists cannot recognise Christians to be good and loyal citizens, not counter-revolutionaries, and to leave them alone to practise their religion freely. But this is precisely what Communists cannot do. Orthodox Communism regards religion, especially the Christian religion, as its bitter enemy and the main obstacle in the way of the attainment of its ultimate goal. Their basic incompatibility is total, despite much common ground."

"I take your point that a Christian cannot be a communist. But surely a Christian does not condemn Communism entirely?"

"To that I would answer that just as you must take the Christian faith as a whole and pass your verdict on it, so you must judge Communism as a whole and pass your verdict. It is not permissible to choose certain aspects of Christian belief and reject others, for the Christian faith is a cohesive whole : it stands or falls together. And it is the same with Communism; it has its system of dogma and no one is free to approve of some aspects and not of others. This was probably the Dean of Canterbury's error : he thought it was possible to select for approval the social and economic theories of Communism, bypass its basic materialism and call oneself a Communist. This was of course a delusion."

"Would you, then, regard the social and economic theories of Communism with any favour?"

"Here I think we are touching on something quite important. We must be quite clear what it is in Communism that is objectionable to a Christian and what there is in it which is both a judgment on the non-Communist world and a challenge to the Church."

"So you do see something good in Communism?"

"Indeed, yes, for I regard Communism as a counterfeit of Christianity!"

"That's intriguing. Tell me in what way."

"Well, first of all, Christianity and Communism have a comparable goal. Like Christianity, Communism espouses the cause of the poor and humble and believes its faith is for all men. The Old Testament prophets predicted an era in earth's history when men would learn war no more, when they would beat their swords into ploughshares, when every man would dwell under his own vine and fig tree and when a King would reign in righteousness—a vision of Christ's future kingdom. Then our Lord taught His disciples to pray 'Thy kingdom come. Thy will be done on earth as it is in heaven.' And the apostles filled in the picture of an earthly reign of Christ. Now the Communists, ever since Karl Marx's prophetic vision of an earthly utopia, have been working to bring about a just society, free from exploitation of man by man, when war would be outlawed and man would be free to devote all his wealth and intellect to harnessing the forces of nature to man's well-being. The difference is that theirs would be a kingdom of man—not of God. But Communism is a faith which holds out a bright promise to men weary with life as it has been in a world of war, hunger, enmity and fear."

"So this explains the great social concern of all Marxists, whether of the Socialist or Communist variety?"

"Yes. And in so far as Communists are genuinely concerned about social justice, the more equitable distribution of wealth and the defence of the under-privileged, Christians must feel a strong bond of sympathy, even though they must also strongly reject the dishonest and violent methods which the orthodox Marxist believes to be essential to change society."

"What is the second point of comparison?"

"I think that the two systems have a comparable view of history. Again, the Old Testament prophets related current

events to the purpose and will of God. They saw God as
active in history. The New Testament eschatology only
underlines the fact that a sovereign God has an eternal plan
which He is now working out in time on this planet—a
plan which will issue in the return of Christ and a new
heaven and a new earth wherein dwelleth righteousness.
Now Dialectical Materialism is regarded as a built-in law
which predetermines the forward movement of society by a
dialectical pathway towards the earthly utopia."

"Yes, I can see the way these two conceptions parallel one
another."

"In the third place, the two systems use comparable
methods . . ."

"Surely not! From all I have heard of brainwashing,
torture, murder, violence practised by Communists, surely
you can't compare these methods with those of Christianity!"

"Are you sure? What about the Crusades with all their
bloodshed? What about the Inquisition and its horrible
tortures? What about the Roman Catholic and Protestant
martyrs in Britain during the reformation and the counter
Reformation? What about the Thirty Years War and all
the other religious wars that have stained the pages of history? Christians should be slow to point the finger at Communists—though this in no way condones the Communists
for their undeniable atrocities. They would argue, though
not using Christian phraseology, that 'before the Millennium
there must be the tribulation'. They claim that before the
perfect human society can emerge there must be the violent
destruction of the old society with all the tribulation. But I
was not really referring to these things when I talked about
methods."

"Sorry for interrupting! Please go on!"

"In the early days of the Communist regime in China,
Communists used methods which were almost identical
with those used by Christians in personal and mass evangelism. They had their inspired Scriptures in the works of
Marx and Lenin. These they expounded in public meetings
and in private study groups. Their aim was to produce a
sense of guilt about the past and a spirit of 'self-criticism'.

This in turn was to be followed by a cleansing of the mind from all wrong ideas (cf. brain-washing) in order to prepare the way for new ideas. And after all the word repentance ('thinking again') has a similar connotation. This in turn was to result in a change which both individuals and churches could experience, to describe which Communists borrowed the Christian term 'new birth'. This, too, was intended to lead to the convert becoming an active propagandist (witness) for his new belief. A Roman Catholic priest in China reports the astonished words of a nun, 'Father, they are using our catechumenate system in order to teach the Communist doctrine!' Confession and penance are zealously practised by all!'"

"How remarkable! And are there any other similarities?"

"Yes—perhaps the most remarkable of all. The two faiths make similar claims! Just as Christianity is a revolutionary religion in that it has the power to change individuals radically and to change home life and society as a whole, so Communists claim to be able to change human nature. What is dynamic in Communism has strong Christian overtones. But while Christians believe that you change society by changing man, Communists believe that you change man by changing the social system. Evil is not, as they see it, in man but in the system. They illustrate their point by demonstrating how in China things like prostitution, theft and corruption have been virtually eliminated by making them economically unnecessary. And they believe that a new race of men will rise from the ashes of the corrupt capitalist civilisation."

"This certainly is an extraordinary claim. And I think I see what you mean by Communism being a counterfeit of Christianity."

"Yes, as I see it, Communism is Satan's masterpiece of deception. As a contributor to *The Spectator* once said, 'The most dangerous antagonists of Christianity have always been those which had some analogy or affinity to it . . . Perhaps the same is true of the strength and the challenge of Communism.' I profoundly disagree therefore with those who see 'the Holy Spirit at work in Communism'. On the contrary, all through Bible history it is possible to trace the record of Satan deceiving men not so much by what is patently evil as by what is apparently good. The first temptation of all was not to commit an immoral act but to taste what was good to look at, good to the taste and likely to bestow wisdom.

"And when you come to think of it, perhaps this is why the badly governed, hungry people of Latin America, Africa and Asia find Communism so attractive. It has so much good to offer. The young admire its realism and desire for social justice. Its success in overcoming political corruption is impressive. The total dedication of its followers to the task of world conquest and their self-sacrifice are unequalled. And its practical economic achievements are great. Is it surprising that in Asia, Africa and Latin America, even Christians are deceived and irritated when missionaries are critical of Communism? But to eat the forbidden fruit will bring certain disaster, and the danger lies in the general ignorance of the consequences for the Christian of Communism in practice. In places like South Africa, where the fear of Communism among white people is almost hysterical, it is very important for Africans to see the whole thing in an objective and balanced way."

"Yes, indeed."

"May I go on to say that socially and economically the achievements of China in twenty years are astounding. Starting almost from scratch and latterly without Russian aid, she has become a nuclear power. As well, she has had resources enough to build a network of railways in the most mountainous and desert terrain of the south-west and north-west as well as elsewhere, to construct vast water conservancy networks and to develop a modern industry. The Chinese were always a nation of expert farmers but up-to-date scientific methods have vastly increased production and ensured a reasonable standard of living for everyone. This in spite of setbacks in 1950–60 and the anarchy of the Cultural Revolution. China rather than India is the envy of other Asian countries. And probably of African countries, too. That is why Asians and Africans alike desperately need to have their eyes opened to the evils of Communism as well as to the material benefits it often brings.

"I would add one other thing. We make a fetish of 'democracy' in the U.S.A. and Europe, particularly of the Western 'one man, one vote' and majority rule ideas which are regarded as the panacea for all evils and the basic rights of all peoples. In fact, western style democracy is probably quite unsuited to Africa or Asia, where paternal government is the traditional pattern and some form of authoritarian rule such as Communism quite acceptable to the people. This is the kind of government which has usually been adopted in Africa once independence has been gained. It also prevails in Asia. We do not therefore criticise Communism because its particular form of democracy is different from our own."

"So you see Communism as a very plausible delusion of Satan! But isn't it equally true to say that it is a tremendous challenge to the Christian Church?"

"Yes, most certainly! Paul Lehmann in the seventh annual 'John Knox Lecture' said, 'Communism is a Christian heresy at an advanced stage of secularisation. Certain goals and values and ideas, central to Christianity, have been appropriated by the Communist movement and transformed into goals and values and ideas central to the achievement of full humanisation by the powers of man alone.' This is what constitutes Communism's supreme challenge."

CHAPTER VI

CHRIST FOR THE MARXIST

THE Marxist is a man or woman for whom Christ died. He is a victim of the one 'who deceiveth the whole world' and the Christian has a duty to present Christ to him as the answer to the human dilemma. Hatred of the system he represents should not allow hatred for the person to intrude at the expense of the constraining love of Christ for men of all sorts. Converts from Communism have usually attributed their conversion to the love of God manifested in the lives of God's people and seldom to being out-argued. Nevertheless, the Christian must be prepared to 'give an answer to every man for the hope that is in him' and to none more than the Marxist whose arguments are so plausible. The missionary working in lands where Communism is a threat also needs to be positive in his teaching to people who, because under-privileged and poorly governed, might be attracted by the promises that Communism holds out.

It would be foolish to deny that we are living in an age of revolution. The twentieth century will certainly go down in history as the century of revolution. There is manifestly something radically wrong with the human race and young people are becoming impatient with the situation. Students all over the world are in revolt against the *status quo*. Spectacular scientific progress is not matched by progress in human relationships. Family relationships, social relationships, race relationships and international relationships are more tragic and more intractable than ever. Christians therefore share with Communists a great concern for the future of mankind. We all long for a solution. But that is as far as we can go together.

The Communist Has No Place for God

Professor Arnold Toynbee says, "Communism is the worship of the collective power of men in place of the worship of God." As Christians therefore we believe the Communist solution to the world's problems to be false primarily because it begins with the wrong assumptions and places a mistaken faith in man's mental powers. To say that man's primary need is food and therefore that the clue to the meaning of history is the struggle to satisfy man's immediate appetites is a false assumption. It is this crude materialism and the denial of all spiritual values to which Christians object. After fifty years the Communist world itself is finding out that revolution is not the only key to the future. Professor J. L. Hromadka of Czechoslovakia, speaking on the fiftieth anniversary of the October Revolution, said that "Social reconstruction is not sufficient for true fulness of life . . . the mere social, economic or political reconstruction does not guarantee the automatic birth of a socialistic person, his growth or the fulness of life. It is interesting to note that intelligent, responsible Communists are occupied with this question to a very great extent today." Ilya Ehrenburg, who won the Lenin Prize in 1944, in his memoirs *People, Years, Life,* Vol. II, wrote : "Man [this is my theological conviction] cannot be explained only in social, economic, political, scientific or technical categories. Man is a certain mystery which surpasses everything which we people have in our hands and which we can dispose of according to our will." The Christian answers that we must first postulate God if we are to understand man. The Russian idealist philosopher, Nicholas Berdyaev, in *The God of Our Time* writes, "Where there is no God there is no man." The world today is hungry for God, for a life that is real, personal and satisfying. Man is a Divine creation, made in the image of God, and consists of both body and soul. St. Augustine's words are relevant here : "Thou madest me for Thyself, and my heart is restless until it find repose in Thee." Within every man there is a 'God-shaped blank' which only God can fill ! Man does not live by bread alone, for his real life derives from God and must be nourished by God. While Marxism stems from a mere rationalistic hypothesis, Christianity is founded on the revelation of a personal God.

The Communist Has a False Concept of Man

The Marxist error in denying God's existence results in a mistaken definition of man. Man, to the Marxist, is purely a social product with his roots in nature. Society, not man, is the real unit in which the individual is merely an element. Man becomes just a cog in a vast soulless machine. The individual is therefore expendable—someone to be used as a means to an end. This surely is exploitation at its worst. By contrast, the concept of man as a Divine creation gives man a dignity denied by the Marxist. Man is not the product of material forces but of God. Nature is made for man, not man for nature. At the same time Christianity does not deny that man is a social being, for the New Testament teaches that man only comes to his full manhood in society, especially in the Christian society of the Church. In Christianity there is no obliterating of the material by the spiritual, while Communism obliterates the spiritual, leaving only the material. It was William Temple who said that "Christianity is the most materialistic religion in the world" because of the Incarnation. Christ dignified manhood by Himself becoming man and so initiating a new race of Christlike men—the redeemed human society. 'What is man?' This marks the real frontier of the world.

The Communist Makes the Fatal Error of Ignoring Sin

When Karl Marx rejected the religion of his Jewish ancestors and the Christian religion of his adoption, he sought in Dialectical Materialism an alternative to the Divine sovereignty in history—a pantheistic concept of the universe and a mechanistic theory of social development which cannot be proved and for which he selected only those evidences which seemed to suit his purpose. His illustrations were from Western Europe and those from the ancient civilisations of the Middle East were ignored. In short, Karl Marx's view of history was too superficial and eclectic, and his description of primitive human society is not supported by anthropologists. The dialectical is not borne out everywhere and no answer is given to the question as to why the dialectical process should stop when the Communist utopia is reached. Logically a new negation, a new antithesis should follow. "In taking God from heaven," says Geoffrey Bull, "the Communist would obliterate any sense of moral obligation to the Creator."

Professor Butterfield of Cambridge University has gone on record as saying that the final effect on him of the reading of history is that "All men are sinners." Sin is the great human factor which cannot be ignored without disaster. It alone is the cause of social and individual disorder. The world's problems are just an extension of our own individual problems. As Aristotle realised, sinful men cannot build a perfect society. Marx and Freud erred in the adoption of the ancient Chinese illusion about man's innate goodness. There is a profound perversity at the roots of human beings and man is therefore helpless alone and stands in need of redemption. The Marxist, by blaming evil on the consequences of an unjust social organisation and the existence of private property, ignores the real origin of evil in the sinful human heart. A doctor who makes such a tragically mistaken diagnosis is not one to be trusted. Only Christ, the Great Physician, discloses the painful truth of the cancer of the soul and offers healing and the creation of a new man through rebirth. A society can only be redeemed through redeemed individuals. "Communism is the mirage of our generation, a quick way to an earthly Paradise." It is but a new version of an ancient folly.

Communism Lacks Any Certainty of Revelation

Karl Marx's *Manifesto* and his subsequent masterpiece *Capital* may have dazzled the poor of the working classes of his day, but both demonstrated the limitations of man's unaided reason which is Communism's only authority. Time has proved his 'surplus value' theory elaborated in *Capital* to be mistaken : under capitalism in Europe and America, the working man, instead of becoming progressively poorer, has enjoyed steadily rising standards of living. Labour did not, as predicted, sink to subsistence level. The mechanisation of industry did not in fact reduce the capitalist's profits. Instead of the two contending classes of Marx's time, at least six classes with varying and not necessarily conflicting interest are identifiable today, so rendering his theory of class struggles and their outcome outmoded. But most important of all, Marx's explanation of the relation of religious, philosophical and ethical ideas to the developing productive power of industry was wrong. The attack on Christianity on these grounds was ill-founded because for two thousand years Christianity has flourished in every age, in different cultures and in many social environments. Though religion has in some cases been used as a weapon in the hands of the ruling class to oppress the working class, this could scarcely be argued of Christianity. Nor can much evidence be adduced today for dismissing Christianity as the opiate of the people : much of the evidence proves the opposite, for the Church in Africa and Asia as well as in Europe has been in the van of social change.

Thus Marx as a prophet has proved to be far from infallible and so undependable as a guide. He was mistaken in his arguments, his economic analysis was unsatisfactory and his historical analysis provides no proof of historic necessity and no solid ground for the claim to be able to forecast the future. So Marxism is partial, inadequate and finally incoherent. "Marx, without knowing it or intending it, revealed the ultimate bankruptcy of mere humanistic thinking at its best" (D. R. Davies).

In the life and teachings of Christ, but especially in His death and resurrection and the fulfilled prophecies of the Old and New Testaments, we have a more sure guide to history and its ultimate consummation in the Kingdom of God. Christ alone is worthy of all confidence. The Bible has stood the test of centuries. It is the rock which has resisted all storms and outlived all criticism.

The Communists Have an Inadequate View of the Future

While it is true to say that the glorious Marxist vision of a world without war, poverty, class or race is dazzling, it must also be called inhuman. For it is to be enjoyed only by those who happen to be alive when the time comes. They alone will enjoy the fruits of the labours, sorrows, struggles, sacrifices and agony of all who have fought for the Marxist revolution. "What can be more callous and monstrous than the idea of a final utopia for a favoured minority of the whole human race?" (D. R. Davies).

How different is the Christian view of a new heaven and a new earth in which righteousness will rule—a heavenly state to be enjoyed by 'a great multitude that no man can number' from every generation—all who have accepted Christ's free offer of salvation. Death is no barrier, for all the righteous and those who have suffered and died will be raised to life : redeemed humanity's fulfilment is not in time but beyond in the great resurrection of the dead. In every generation, the Christian has had the privilege of working with God in doing His will. All will share in the final triumph of God's purposes.

These are a few of the weapons in the Christian's armoury. In our dialogue we should agree with the Marxist as to some of our common goals—particularly the need for justice, peace and good government, and so establish a good initial understanding. As far as possible, we should avoid all negative and antagonistic attitudes. Then we must clearly define the common problem, for 'a problem well stated is half solved'. Finally, while admitting the necessity for historic basic assumptions, we need to emphasise the necessity to distinguish between facts and their interpretation.

Having gone so far, we must always defend our basic premises—the origin of the universe and of man, the true nature of man, the fact of the historic Christ and the essential distinction between right and wrong. We may well make our point effectively by asking questions such as : "Can you prove that war and violence ever produce peace?" "How do you know that the dialectical process is absolute?" "What makes you think that man can control his own destiny?" "Can you prove that good negates itself?"

In short, "the problems posed by Communism are ultimately religious. The practical problems are moral, the theoretical problems are theological". (*A Christian Commen-*

tary on Communism by Edward Rogers) Christianity is realistic. It confronts the problem of original sin, the only answer to which is the sole right of Christ to forgive sins and His power to change human nature. Filled with the love of Christ, we must be prepared to declare God's remedy to Marxists everywhere – whether in our own universities and in industrial circles or among the ardent followers of Communism in Europe, China or Russia itself.

CHAPTER VII

UNTO CAESAR

A YEAR after Mao announced the foundation of the People's Republic, Prime Minister Chou En-lai invited the Church leaders to Peking to dictate the Party's terms of survival for the Church. The Church, he insisted, must rid itself of all traces of imperialism, meaning, primarily, the missionaries and the money supplied by 'imperialist' nations to the churches. The Church was also asked to accept the leadership of the Communist Party. The leaders—though not at all representative of all the churches—agreed. Thus the Christian Church placed itself firmly under State control. This control was exercised by the Religious Affairs Bureau which controlled the affairs of all religions in China. For the easier management of Protestant affairs, the R.A.B. set up the Three Self Patriotic Movement. Eventually even the most reluctant Christian groups saw no alternative to joining this organisation.

The Christian press began to pay tribute to the achievements of the People's Government. Marx, Lenin and Mao were compared to the Old Testament prophets and the new society in China to the Kingdom of God. The paper *Tien Feng* became the official mouthpiece of Communist policies related to the Church and was used in all its campaigns against those Christians who refused to follow the Party line. Right up to the time of the Church's temporary extinction in 1966 by the Cultural Revolution, spokesmen and writers continued to give loyal support to the Government, to protest their freedom under the People's Government and to declare the wholehearted patriotism of the movement and its opposition to American imperialism in particular. In spite of this, the Red Guards closed the churches, insulted and maltreated countless Christians, carried away many of the Church leaders and liquidated the Three Self Patriotic Movement.

This experience demands a fresh examination of the duties and responsibilities, the obligations and loyalties of Christians who face the prospect of living or must continue to live under an authoritarian, an anti-Christian and a Communist regime. Some leaders and some members may succeed in escaping the country either before or after a Communist takeover, but the majority of Christians will always perforce have to remain to face the music.

In 64 A.D., as the empire-wide persecution under the Emperor Nero was about to break over the heads of the Christians, the Apostle Peter wrote his first Epistle. In it he first of all emphasised the great foundation truths of the Gospel and then insisted that the ultimate Christian answer to persecutors, detractors and critics is that of a blameless life, conduct beyond reproach and good citizenship. "Now who is he that will harm you if you are zealous for what is right?" (1 Peter 3 :13 R.S.V.). "Keep your conscience clear" (1 Peter 3 :16 R.S..V). "Let none of you suffer as ... a wrong doer" (1 Peter 4 :15 R.S.V.). But in particular, Peter uses the injunction "Be subject" four times and in four different contexts : in the church (1 Peter 5 :5), in the family (1 Peter 3 :1), in society (1 Peter 2 :18) and in the state (1 Peter 2 :13). Submission is a supremely Christlike virtue.

When we realise that many Christians were in fact slaves, it is highly significant that neither Peter nor Paul said anything to suggest that they should seek freedom by political action (1 Peter 2 :18-25). Peter counsels slaves to submit even to bad, cruel and unjust masters and uses the unjust sufferings of Christ as an example. In this he does not condone slavery, but he does spell out a Christian's proper attitude even in an unjust and unequal society.

In the context of the state, Peter writes, "Be subject for the Lord's sake to every human institution, whether it be to the emperor (Nero) as supreme or to governors ... for it is God's will that by doing right you should put to silence the ignorance of foolish men ... Fear God. Honour the emperor (1 Peter 2 :13–17). Such advice must have been hard to take for Christians suffering directly on account of Nero's wicked and false accusation that it was they who set fire to Rome and not Nero himself. Yet the principle is clearly stated : namely, that Christians are not to rebel against any government just because it is dictatorial, authoritarian or corrupt. Not only must they give respect to the representatives of government as those who represent the law (v. 14) but they are to submit to the decrees and laws of that government and so live "as servants of God" (v. 16).

The Apostle Paul, in the Epistle to the Romans, after ten chapters of treatise concerning the Gospel, turns in Chapter XI to the practical application of these truths. He describes the Christian life in the church (v. 3–8), his personal conduct (v. 9–13), his attitude under persecution (v. 14–21) and then in Chapter XIII he broaches the very difficult matter of the Christian and the State. But what he says is similar to what Peter said, though considerably amplified. While St. Peter spoke about the divinely-ordained function of government, St. Paul lays stress on the divine origin of the State. The injunction in both cases is identical – "Be in subjection to the governing authorities" (v. 1) as the representatives of law (v. 3, 4). The reasons are then given : (1) all authority has been instituted of God (v. 1); (2) the Christian sins if he resists that authority (v. 2); (3) subjection must be a matter of conscience and not just because of fear of Divine punishment. In particular, the Christian citizen is obliged to pay his taxes, dues and revenues and to respect and honour the responsible officials. Thus the Christian is confronted with (1) the duty of civil obedience; (2) the reason for civil obedience; and (3) the spirit of civil obedience. Placed in the context of the Roman Empire, an alien power often guilty of exorbitant taxation and unjust demands, these inspired instructions must have caused much heart scarching in the early Church.

But both Paul's and Peter's instructions about the proper attitudes and conduct of Christians in relation to the State are based on Our Lord's reply to those who sought to involve Him in treason with the Roman Government (Luke 20 :20). His devastating reply was so unexpected that the scribes could only marvel (v. 26) – "Render unto Caesar the things that are Caesar's and unto God the things that are

God's" even though everyone was groaning under the heavy taxation imposed by the Emperor Tiberius. This answer embodies the general principle that "Government has rightful claims over its citizens, but not ultimate claims. Only God has ultimate claims. The issues over which these claims come into conflict vary from country to country and time to time e.g. the concentration camps in Nazi Germany and the civil rights problem of North America. The issues even vary from Christian to Christian, for one will sense a powerful conflict over an issue that another fails to see as an issue. Jesus does not give detailed instructions to resolve every possible conflict of loyalties. But the Christian must do the best he can to know the issues in his circumstances, to sort out his loyalties and to serve God in good conscience. If this involves him in conflict with the State or public opinion, he may suffer eventual loss of privilege, property or even life." (Scripture Union notes by Rev. A. Warren Hutchins, B.A., B.D.) As Peter said, in effect, "But even if you do suffer for righteousness sake, you will be blessed . . .'

God is a God of order and not of confusion. He has therefore appointed civil government for the general good of mankind. They are indeed an ordinance of God (Rom. 13 :1). "Nothing could be clearer than St. Peter's conviction that in the purpose of God society is to bear on its face the impress of the Divine order" (G. W. D. Addleshaw). Now the governments of New Testament times were not 'Christian governments' as we call ours in the West today. They were undemocratic and pagan. Nevertheless it is through God's providential dealings with men that they are advanced to places of authority (Psalm 75 :6, 7) where they rightly command obedience and loyalty. They may be dictators, but even then such rule is better than anarchy unless it has been utterly evil and oppressive : in which case Christians are absolved from the duty of obedience, just as a child is absolved from obeying a vicious parent, though in normal circumstances it is bound to obey. With all their failings and shortcomings, few governments are utterly bad; most have some good in them. But whether the governments be good or bad, the New Testament writers insisted that civil obedience, whenever consistent with a good conscience, is a Christian duty and it is urged on Christians as that which is conformable to the will of God. Christians all down the ages have been slandered for rebellion against the State and one of the commonest prejudices that the world has against true religion is that religion is the enemy of the State.

Clearly, therefore, it is a Christian duty under any regime —Buddhist, Hindu, Muslim, Communist or Christian—to be a good and obedient citizen in all civil concerns. A Christian may or may not fully agree with the policies and laws of his government; nevertheless he is duty bound to submit to the authorities in everything that does not concern his religious convictions, except where the laws clearly contravene the will of God. Christians all over the world today find themselves living under bad, corrupt or inefficient governments as well as under efficient but authoritarian and dictatorial governments. Nevertheless, "It cannot consist with submission to the providence of God to attempt the illegal and violent subversion of any existing government or to engage in any form of civil disobedience." The Taiping Rebellion, hailed by the Communists as a peasant uprising, had Christian inspiration behind it. But this rebellion against the State was a travesty of true Christianity and cannot be justified by any standards at all. The New Testament never represents Christ or the Church as hostile to the State, though it recognises the paradox that the Christian, though in the world, is not of it. He has a dual citizenship—of an earthly state and of a heavenly kingdom. Christ, Paul and Peter all agree that they must submit themselves to authority and not flout it. The Lord Himself provides an example of submission before Pilate for His disciples to follow. This must be the pattern in China, in Russia, in Eastern Europe, in Cuba, or in the United States where Christian Negroes are faced with grave problems. The only legitimate action suggested in the New Testament is that enjoined in 1 Tim. 2 : 1; if he would live a quiet and peaceful life in godliness and honesty, the Christian must pray for the authorities. It would be difficult both to pray for and to rebel against those authorities at the same time.

So far so good. But what about religious issues? It is here that the greatest tensions arose in the early Church. In those days the state was conceived as the highest good and so everything, including religion, had to be subordinate to it. But in fact Christians—without exception and therefore by common agreement, presumably—refused to worship the Emperor. They also refused to obey the local Jewish religious authorities in Jerusalem and refrain from preaching the Gospel (Acts 5 :29). But perhaps this was slightly different, as disobedience to *civil* authorities was not involved.

The situation was complicated by the Roman laws forbidding the practice of new religions and secret associations. "These men are Jews and they are disturbing our city. They advocate customs which it is not lawful for us Romans to accept or practise" (Acts 16 :20, 21 R.S.V.). The secrecy of some of their gatherings, particularly the Lord's Supper, laid the Christians open to suspicion. Furthermore their religious convictions and desire to maintain high moral standards led them to withdraw from social, business and political associations connected in any way with heathen customs. Separation from evil and refusal to be intimately yoked with unbelievers in marriage or business often created a dilemma for the early Christians. What was clear was that while the Christian may submit his body to Caesar, his conscience and faith he cannot submit. In certain circumstances disobedience to the command of the State may be not only a right but a duty. The New Testament writers, especially Peter, make it clear that faithfulness to principle here would inevitably involve Christians in trouble, in persecution and even in death. So Peter says, "Arm yourselves likewise with the same mind" as Christ who was prepared to die (1 Peter 4 :1)—that is, be prepared to die for your faith if necessary.

In Russia during the Tsarist times, some State control of the Church existed. Then under Lenin the Church was in a position of separation from the State. Under Stalin the Church was tolerated so long as it bowed the knee to authority. For the first few years after Stalin's death there was no clear religious policy, but as soon as Khruschev had established his authority in 1959–60, local Communist authorities with higher authority began to dismantle the visible structure of the Church by force and in defiance of the law. In 1961 (as reported by Michael Bourdeaux in the *Church Times*, March 22, 1968), with less than twenty-four hours' notice, the Patriarch Alexeis called a Council of Bishops for a formal synod to be asked to approve a new list of regulations with hardly any formal discussion. The decisions were then foisted on the churches in an ill-considered way and violently removed the control of parish life from the clergy and handed it over to a lay council of twenty-four men acceptable to the Party. Thus and out-and-out atheist control of the churches was substituted for autonomous control and the disbanding of the churches proceeded. At least 50 per cent of Russia's 20,000 Orthodox churches were closed.

In one diocese, however, none were closed — the Tashkent diocese where Archbishop Yermogen refused to close a single church. For this he suffered a year's eclipse. In 1965 he led a delegation of eight bishops to see the Patriarch, only to be rebuffed. Moreover, on the request of the Chairman of the Council on Religious Affairs of the Council of Ministers of the U.S.S.R. Archbishop Yermogen was 'persuaded' to retire. The following year two Moscow priests published an open letter of protest and sent copies to every bishop : these evoked considerable sympathy but led to a ban on both priests from office. But Archbishop Yermogen had not been silenced. He refused to dissociate himself from the position of the two priests and has continued to demand that the Patriarch should fulfil his promise to give him a diocese as soon as one became vacant. In November 1967 Archbishop Yermogen appealed to the Patriarch to insist on the legal separate status of the Church according to the 1929 codification of laws. The Patriarch is ninety and the question of his successor must be in the minds of all Orthodox Christians in Russia, of whom there are thirty million. Undoubtedly the State will want to appoint its own nominee who would be subservient to the Government. But under the leadership of Archbishop Yermogen a strong body of opinion is demanding a new meeting of the House of Bishops to set the Church's house in order. He takes courage from the example of the Russian Baptists who have won from the Government the right to hold an All Union Congress every three years. Thus Baptists and Orthodox are demanding a return to the rule of law. "The voice of Archbishop Yermogen is a warning not only to the whole Church but also to the Soviet Government." Great issues of religious liberty are at stake.

But what of China? Certain facts are clear. Unlike the early Church, the Chinese Church lacked a strong united leadership; it was not able, when a Communist government was set up, to speak with one voice and act together to refuse 'emperor (or state) worship'; it had not reached agreement on the implications of our Lord's words, "Render unto Caesar the things that are Caesar's, and unto God the things that are God's". Consequently the Religious Affairs Bureau had little difficulty in imposing its will on the Protestant churches although it met with stronger opposition from the Roman Catholic Church, which enjoyed more resolute leadership and had well formulated principles. It was therefore comparatively easy to pursue its policy of rendering the Protestant churches ineffective, apparently irrelevant and impotent through the subtle manipulation by the Three Self Patriotic Movement.

In Czechoslovakia, Alexander Dubcek's liberalisation policies in early 1968 caused Christians to rejoice in a freedom from controls they had not known for twenty years. The future looked bright with hope. In Rumania where people were desirous of a similar kind of liberalisation, the Government authorised the printing of a large edition of the Bible. On April 5th, 1968, the *Daily Telegraph* forecast for Czechoslovakia, though still under a one-party Communist Government, an upsurge of spiritual freedom, a relaxation of police controls, a freer press and considerable right of open protest.

But in Russia the so-called 'liberalisation' was denounced as counter-revolution which constituted a challenge to Marxist orthodoxy, a threat to the Warsaw Pact alliance and a potential sword pointed at the Ukraine itself. And on August 21st, the Warsaw Pact countries under Russian instructions treacherously invaded Czechoslovakia. Communist Parties around the world denounced the invasion and felt deep sympathy towards the people and the Communist Party of Czechoslovakia and its liberalising aims.

Communist China, while condemning the invasion, also condemned Dubcek's 'liberalising' or 'revisionist' heresy which, China claimed, Czechoslovakia had learned from Russia. Professor Hromadka, the Czech Christian leader, protested strongly to the Soviet embassy about Russia's action and at the same time appealed to all Christians to maintain a Christian dignity and solidarity in the face of the changed situation. Nevertheless, with the occupation of their country by foreign troops, the Czechs must anticipate the future with foreboding unless the Russians experience a change of heart.

The Communist world is in discord. The upsurge of revolt against Stalinist tyranny is so powerful that the day must come when even Russian tanks and planes will be helpless to stand in its way. Czechoslovakia and other Russian satellites will yet know freedom. And should the time come when liberal policies prevail in China and constitutional freedom be restored to the Christian Church there, one would fervently hope and pray that the example of Russian and Czechoslovakian churches will be noted and that Chinese Christians will reject the former government-imposed strait-jacket and demand genuine freedom to conduct their own church affairs and to pursue their religious life without state interference.

CHAPTER VIII

CRITICISM AND SELF-CRITICISM

In 1950, the Chinese Communists launched their attack on Christian missions and Christian missionaries. For eighteen years the campaign of vilification has continued, in an endeavour to discredit the missionary contribution utterly. The missionary movement has been accused of all sorts of crimes so consistently that even the Chinese Church must sometimes have been persuaded of the truth. Indeed Y. T. Wu and other leading Christians have clearly expressed these views in the national press and in their public statements.

It is right that, instead of merely denying these accusations, we who served in China should face the criticisms, analyse them and see how far they contain any degree of truth. Honesty is the least thing required of us and self-criticism is no Communist monopoly.

The criticisms can be summarised under seven heads :

i. The 'Missionary Enterprise' has from the first been the instrument of colonial expansion in foreign lands and was inseparable from imperialist policies and aggression.

ii. Missionaries were employed by imperialist governments to assist them in their aggression.

iii. Missionaries used money to buy and to enslave Chinese Christians to collaborate with them. Thus the Church was the tool of imperialism.

iv. Missionaries taught doctrines which were nothing less than imperialist poison in the minds of those who accepted them.

v. Missionaries used schools and Sunday Schools to corrupt young minds with imperialism : the schools were consequently hotbeds of reactionary propaganda.

vi. Missionaries dominated and controlled the churches in an imperialistic fashion.

    vii. Missionaries used denominational differences as a device to divide and rule.

We should consider each of these in turn—sympathetically and honestly :

i. *The 'Missionary Enterprise' has from the first been the instrument of colonial expansion in foreign lands and was inseparable from imperialist policies and aggression.*

Looked at from the point of view of a non-Christian African or Asian this is true. Historically, the expansion of Christianity throughout the world has paralleled the imperialist and colonialist expansion of the West. In the case of Africa, David Livingstone, the missionary, pioneered the vast interior, and colonial governments followed. In the case of China, treaties imposed on China as a sequel to the Opium Wars (the 'Unequal Treaties') exacted the right of foreign merchants to live and trade in China and thereby opened the way for the entrance of missionaries bearing the good news of Christ for all men. Books like *Missionaries, China and Diplomats* (Paul Vary, 1958) seem to confirm the suspicions of the Communists. From a Christian point of view the coming of the Gospel to China was wholly a good thing, even though it happened to come on the heels of the merchants. However, it is easy to see how, from Sun Yat-sen to Mao Tse-tung, the coincidence has been mistakenly interpreted as if Christian missions and missionaries were an integral part of the imperialist programme of expansion. The coincidence is unfortunate but the interpretation put on it by the enemies of Christianity is false. History has been rewritten in China in order to show the missionary movement there in the worst possible light.

ii. *Missionaries were employed by imperialist governments to assist them in their aggression.*

Most Chinese Christians found it hard to believe that missionaries were not directly employed and paid by their governments. No amount of denial could persuade them to the contrary. The corollary was that missionaries were all engaged in political or cultural activities in the cause of imperialism. This was utterly false. Missionaries in the early days were actually unwelcome by their government representatives and the British House of Commons protested about their presence in China. None ever received direct or indirect payment from governments, but they were supported by the voluntary sacrificial giving of Christian people all over the world. The accusation was usually due to ignorance but sometimes to malice. Some actions and attitudes which, in the contemporary situation of the time, were innocent enough can now by interpreted in the light of present-day nationalism as suspicious if not subversive. But it is unfair to apply present-day criteria to actions which took place fifty or more years ago. That missionaries were employed by the American Central Intelligence Agency is demonstrably untrue, even though isolated individuals may have been false to their calling, just as some missionaries became agents of Communism.

iii. *Missionaries used money to buy and enslave Chinese Christians to collaborate with them. Thus the Church was the tool of imperialism.*

Missionaries undoubtedly used large sums of money to train and to support Chinese Christians in their work as pastors, evangelists, church workers, teachers, doctors, colporteurs, administrators etc. In so doing they unwittingly and unfortunately placed such people in the position of being 'running dogs of the imperialists' in the eyes of post-World War I anti-Christian nationalists and Communists. However, the use of mission funds had no ulterior motives. They were used for the sole purpose of building up the Church and spreading the Gospel. But naturally, the control of funds gave to missionaries real control in many ways. Missionaries have, it is hoped, learned their lessons in the thorny matter of the administration of mission funds. Money from foreign sources donated to native churches is nearly always a millstone around the church's neck—a grave hindrance to progress.

iv. *Missionaries taught doctrines which were nothing less than imperialist poison in the minds of those who accepted them.*

A close investigation of these alleged poisonous doctrines revealed that they were doctrines which did not fit in with Communist ideology; viz., all men are sinners, man cannot save himself, the state of society is growing worse, the times are becoming darker, Christ is coming again to bring in His reign of righteousness and peace, etc. Seeing that such ideas run contrary to Communist dogma, they were labelled 'poison'. But Christian ideas which happen to be in opposition to those of Marxism–Leninism are poison only to Communists : to others they are the bread and the water of life.

v. *Missionaries used schools and Sunday Schools to corrupt young minds with imperialism: the schools were consequently hotbeds of reactionary propaganda.*

Missionaries certainly used schools to provide a good education for the children of Christian families and for non-Christians, too, if they chose to attend. The truths of Christianity were taught and, after 1911 Nationalist Revolution, a curriculum based on that of the West was adopted. This was by the universal demand of the Chinese people themselves. Missions are not ashamed of the major contribution they have made to modern education in China, of which they were the pioneers. If, at times, there was a temptation to think that spreading a western culture and way of life was a part of the missionary's task, then they acted only in the belief – sometimes mistaken – that this was best for the Chinese people. Sunday Schools were certainly not 'a dishonourable system harmful to children' and their curriculum contained no political teaching though, of course, much that was taught to children would be in conflict with Communist ideology.

vi. *Missionaries dominated and controlled the churches in an imperialistic fashion.*

Here, few would deny the truth of the accusation. Initially missionaries brought with them to China superior knowledge, experience and character and they automatically assumed the leadership within the Christian community. Generally speaking, the Chinese accepted the situation as quite natural. But it is now clearly seen and freely admitted that missionaries clung to their authority far too long and failed to entrust leadership and responsibility to the able potential leaders of the Chinese churches. The attitude of missionaries towards the Chinese was often condescending, patronising and paternal, and sometimes even offensively arrogant. When they should have been 'servants' they too often behaved as masters, until, almost too late, they realised their mistake.

vii. *Missionaries used denominational differences as a device to divide and rule.*

In spite of early attempts, such as that made by the London Missionary Society, to form missionary societies free of denominational bias, the conscience about 'our sins of division' was not so sensitive a hundred years ago as it is today. It seemed quite natural, even unavoidable, to export denominationalism with the Gospel. In the light of history it is easy to see the confusion this action has caused and still causes. But to say that missionaries deliberately used denominations to maintain their control of the churches is patently mistaken.

To sum up—while there are factors which enable ill-intentioned people and enemies of the Gospel to justify the accusation that missionaries have been imperialist agents and are still a part of an imperialist plot to control the churches, an impartial judge, having considered all the facts, would reject the broad accusation as totally untrue as far as China was concerned. In India and Africa the work of missions and the work of colonial governments were much more inextricably associated and it would be harder to make such a categorical denial. That missionaries carried with them the ideas and cultural traditions associated with the 'imperialist' West, especially in the Victorian era, was inevitable, but in no sense did they consciously propagate imperialism while in recent decades there has been a steady reversal of earlier tendencies.

.   .   .   .   .

But we who went as Christian missionaries to China under many organisations and from a variety of theological backgrounds are prepared, not only to listen to the criticism of our Chinese colleagues, but to add our own humble self-criticism. And thus WE CONFESS to our Chinese friends :

I. *that too many of us were guilty of preaching a diluted Christian Gospel:*
Some of us had no Gospel at all except one of good works,

although Confucius and Buddha taught as clearly as any of us the necessity for ethical living. Some of us knew only a Gospel of self-improvement, physically and morally. Many of us had no experience of the saving and transforming power of the crucified and risen Lord Jesus Christ in our own lives. We did not believe the Bible to be the Word of God and we shared with you our disbelief and undermined your faith. We did not rely upon the miracle-working power of the Holy Spirit, but solely upon our own education, ability and methods. Our building was of wood, hay and stubble which the fire has consumed. Only the ashes remain.

ii. *that too many of us remained grossly ignorant of your culture, literature and thought:*

As one of you has rightly said, "The man who is a missionary is nearly always a stranger to the country where he works. At heart he must be. Some who came to China ceased to be foreign to us. We remember them with great love." "Yes, we were strangers in your midst. Many of you knew our classics, but few of us knew yours. Your natural insight into character helped you to read us, but we found you inscrutable. We failed to understand you. Thus we failed to communicate the Gospel in relevant terms and it remained 'a foreign religion'—not like Buddhism which, though also a foreign religion, found the secret of becoming Chinese. No wonder so few of you believed. No wonder the Church was so small, so weak, so open to criticism as an alien culture.

iii. *that too many of us were reluctant to identify ourselves with you:*

We knew in theory that we ought to be identified with you but we shrank from too close identification. Even though we adopted some forms of external identification, our real lives were miles apart. Our love was insufficient to break through the barriers between us. We professed to love your souls, but we failed to love you as people. You didn't know us intimately and we didn't know you, though we were on polite, friendly terms. We clung to our western standards of living and were unwilling to give them up. We still wanted to keep our way of life rather than adopt yours. So we built walled compounds from which you were often excluded. Even our homes and our guest rooms were not for you to share. And you were justifiably grieved about this.

iv. *that we were too possessive to allow your free development:*

We clung to our authority. We were your spiritual parents. You were our children. We didn't let you grow up to enjoy the freedom you needed to make you strong and independent. We didn't trust you as Paul trusted his converts and the Holy Spirit in them. We failed to emphasise the training of a virile and robust national leadership. We even resented your independent church movements because they seemed to damage our work and hurt us. In spite of this, you did develop independent churches and produced many outstanding leaders. How different things might have been if we had done more! We see our mistakes only too clearly.

v. *that we were too preoccupied with our institutions and too little concerned with planting strong local churches:*

Because we brought you the first hospitals and the first schools, we made a fetish of them. They absorbed most of our personnel and used up most of our funds. Not that education and medicine were wrong, but they should have been secondary to the task of evangelising and planting local churches which would grow in strength and effectiveness. Now we have seen the institutions taken over by your Government. And what was left? Only the churches. And we found how weak and leaderless they really were—almost ready to collapse at the first onslaught. Too often the weakest churches were those in places where the biggest institutions were to be found—overshadowed by hospital or school and their organisation monopolised by the employees in the institutions. We failed to see our priorities, and the failure of your churches under Communist pressures is our failure.

vi. *that we neglected to prepare you for the advent of a Communist government:*

We seldom discussed social and political issues from the Biblical point of view. We were not very sure ourselves what we believed about Church and State, so we kept quiet—criminally quiet. And when the crunch came you were found wanting—uncertain, bewildered, without convic-

tions, disunited. We neglected our duty toward you in this
respect. And you have suffered from our neglect.

vii. *that we were too unconcerned about social justice and
lacking in social concern.*

We said this was no concern of ours. We needed only to
preach the Gospel so that people would be saved. But we
overlooked the warnings of the Old Testament prophets
and the commands of the New Testament writers relating
to social duties and obligations. We saw your poverty, witnessed the injustices, the corruption and the oppression, but
generally speaking we kept silent. We knew well that social
action is a by-product of true Christian faith, but failed to
speak against the evils of society as Wesley and Wilberforce
did. We did not do enough for the outcast, the orphans and
the widows. Our Gospel was so often devoid of social application. And we therefore laid ourselves open to the Communist taunt that Christianity is little more than an opiate to
relieve the pain without dealing with the cause.

vii. *that we sadly neglected to provide you with adequate
Christian literature:*

We gave you tracts and booklets. But of the books we
translated or wrote, many met no real need and had a path-
etically small circulation. Those that met a deep need found
a ready market, but they were few. It was possible to collect
only a dozen or so worthwhile paper-backs to send out to
your pastors as personal libraries before we left China. We
gave you too few commentaries, dictionaries, concordances,
books on apologetics, history, heresies, ethics, devotion.
Now we are trying to make up for lost time. Perhaps one
day—God knows—you will have a worthy library of scholarship and devotion to replace those you have recently lost.

We are sure there were many other faults, omissions and
sins. But these we confess with deep sincerity. Perhaps one
day—God willing—we will be permitted to make amends.

CHAPTER IX

RETURN TO CHINA

CHINA is a nation and the Chinese a race which cannot be ignored. They will increasingly play a prominent role in world affairs. For better or for worse our future and especially that of our children and grandchildren will be affected by the course of events in China. The ancient culture, the outstanding ability, the numerous skills, the industry, the vast resources, the adaptability, and the sheer weight of numbers of the Chinese people make them probably the greatest race on earth. Their traditional tolerant humanism could be an influence contributing to the harmony and well-being of the world. On the other hand, the passionate hatreds, the slavish subservience to an alien creed and the irresponsible leadership which Communism has produced now constitute a serious threat to the rest of the world—especially since China has become a nuclear power.

China Watchers

'China Watchers' in Hong Kong disagree about the future of the Church of Jesus Christ in China. Some fear it is virtually being destroyed as the churches in North Africa and in Asia Minor were in the first century, including such strong churches as Ephesus, Smyrna and Philadelphia. Others are optimistic about the future of the Chinese Church and foresee a time when a limited re-entry into China by Chinese and other Asians will be possible. Some, however, are of the opinion that only Chinese who have experienced the Revolution will be able to minister to their people and that the days of the Westerner and even of the Western trained and orientated Chinese are definitely over. On the other hand, there are also those who feel that we must prepare for any eventuality, including the return of Western Christian workers to China.

Moreover, China, where a quarter of the human race lives, is the biggest and most strategic unevangelised region in the world. But the doors into China are now firmly closed and the Chinese Church is totally isolated from the Church elsewhere. At present, the prospect of sending aid to the Chinese Church is, humanly speaking, remote. Although the turmoil in China, amounting at times to civil war, has stirred hopes in 'Free China' (or Taiwan) that the collapse of Communism is imminent and a Nationalist return to the mainland within sight such wishful thinking overlooks the fact that the current 'struggle' is not one between Communists and anti-Communists, but an ideological 'struggle' between different factions of Communism, and related to the leading personalities of the Communist Party. 'Struggle' is integral to Communist ideology and caution is needed in predicting the outcome of the current chaos. Nevertheless nothing is impossible with God!

Possible Liberalisation

If events proceed in the traditional Chinese way, moderation and the practical common sense of the Chinese will ultimately prevail against extremist dogmatism. Mao Tsetung's successor will almost certainly represent the more intellectual, moderate faction in Chinese Communism which desires a rapid modernisation of the economy and the armed forces, probably with Russian assistance. Such a new regime might conceivably restore the constitutional liberty of religious bodies in China as with Czechoslovakia after the January 1968 liberalisation under Dubcek. Church buildings may yet be handed back to Christians and church life restored again, as Mrs. Strong (cf. p. 43) has predicted. It is perhaps significant that the Three Self Movement Committee remains in existence on paper. It could be resuscitated—wiser, perhaps, under different leadership, free from government domination and with a more positively Christian programme than before. The future may even yet provide tremendous opportunities for the Church of Jesus Christ. If it does, that Church will be confronted with the greatest evangelistic challenge in history.

Who Will Return?

Should these hopes be realised, the Chinese Church will need all the aid that sister churches overseas can provide and will no doubt welcome back to the mainland the hundreds of Chinese Christians in Hong Kong, Taiwan and elsewhere, who have been preparing themselves for such a possibility. May not the existence of so many people with this vision be a token that God has heard their prayers and will open the doors to the mainland again? Besides Chinese a welcome would doubtless be extended to other Asians—Koreans, Japanese, Indonesians, Indians, etc. Since 1950, the Chinese people have become familiar with the coming and going of 'foreign guests' from all over the world in large numbers and 'Christian' guests from other Asian countries would not be at all conspicuous in the New China.

But a welcome for Americans by the Chinese people in general must be regarded as only a distant possibility: twenty years of instilled hatred for the so-called 'U.S. imperialists', the bitterness aroused by the Vietnam war, the U.S. protection of Taiwan and the racial strife in the U.S.A. have completely alienated Americans from the Chinese people as a whole. Canada and Great Britain have maintained diplomatic relations with China, while Australia and New Zealand are in somewhat better favour with Peking than other 'western' nations, but the welcome back to China of British Commonwealth nationals would not be enthusiastic.

A Planned Return

However, just for the sake of argument, if the doors of China were suddenly and dramatically to swing open, let us ask ourselves : Is the Christian Church prepared? Have we a well-thought-out policy or plan? What task force is being trained? In what situation would we find ourselves? How would we go about communicating the Gospel in a radically changed China? What past errors would we seek to avoid? These are questions of more than academic interest: they are of the utmost importance if we believe that God has not cast off the seven hundred to eight hundred million people of China. Such questions need to be prayerfully discussed and appropriate action taken. It would be criminal to be caught unprepared as the Christian Church was in the case of Japan after the last war. And how tragic it would be to let loose on a suspicious, even hostile Chinese population a motley horde of ill-prepared, ill-equipped, disorganised and blundering, if enthusiastic, 'missionaries'—Asians, Americans, Europeans! The thought of hundreds of societies all flying different pennants and using different shibboleths walking into the Communist tiger's lair makes the mind boggle! How prepared then is the Church?

An Unrecognisable China

Is it possible, first of all, to picture the kind of China we should find—that is, when the present disorders resulting from the Cultural Revolution come to an end? It would be a China as different from the one which missionaries left in 1951 as Britain in 1968 differs from Britain in 1868. Progress which has required several generations in the West has been crowded into a single generation in China: progress in industry, agriculture, education, communications, building, engineering, public health and social welfare has been dramatic. The new China is in many ways almost unrecognisable. During the past few years many centres of Chinese study have been set up throughout Europe and in Asia. And Christians cannot afford to be behind others in their studies of Chinese society, the Chinese economy and China's foreign relations if they are to understand what is happening to Chinese Christians on the mainland and what conditions anyone returning to China would find.

Six Facts to Ponder

i. We should find greatly increased efficiency and order, cleanliness and discipline: all visitors to China, whether business men, scientists or churchmen, are impressed with the contrasts between China today and the old China of inefficiency and *laissez-faire*. Government education, public health and welfare organisations have taken over or replaced all missionary institutions which will find no further place. Whatever Christians may take back to China, it will not be just philanthropy, social welfare or charity. This institutional type of contribution has gone for ever.

ii. After twenty years of intensive indoctrination, we should find the minds of all the people, even Christians, to have been profoundly affected. Their political and international outlook will be narrow, seeing that they have been denied objective information and free discussion. Propaganda has been the most effective of New China's industries.

iii. We should meet a fierce hatred of the United States and other 'imperialist' countries, which are accused of being behind all the world's evils and of being the main barrier to the realisation of a new social order based on justice. As 'imperialists' even our motives in returning to China would be gravely suspect.

iv. Most of us would find understanding the newspapers more difficult than ever : for one thing, the Chinese have adopted a new simplified script which is not easy to read without study. But to make things more difficult, in the People's Republic everyday terms, idioms and vocabulary have undergone great changes. A new Communist jargon is in common use. The language of the people in the street has so changed that normal communication would at first be very difficult. It would be a slow process to reach a meeting place of minds.

v. Among the children, the 'tall' noses of Westerners would attract the same old comments ! But, in other ways, too, we would seem like people from a different planet. The younger Chinese have been conditioned by Dialectical Materialism almost from the cradle. They have known no other philosophy than materialism. We would therefore find most of them to be atheists despising Christians as simpletons and unscientific 'backward elements'. The 'generation gap' would be far more pronounced than any we meet in the West and the gulf well-nigh impossible to bridge.

vi. But we should also find that superstition, ancestor worship and idolatry—things once such an obstacle to the progress of the Gospel—had been dealt a death blow.

Thus socially, intellectually, religiously and psychologic-
ally we would be confronted with a situation which could
be met only through the wisdom and power of God granted
to His servants. Anyone inadequately prepared would suffer
severe 'culture shock' before many weeks had passed. The
task would be a formidable one, but, led by the Spirit of
God who is always sufficient for any situation, Christians
would not be daunted by the mountainous difficulties. Evangelicals should be praying together, planning together and
training a thoroughly equipped international force ready to
move as soon as the time is ripe.

Ten Guide Lines for Consideration

i. *The return to China should not be a mission-centred
but church-based enterprise.* No foreign missionary society
or board as such should seek to return on a society basis.
There must be no repetition of the multiple society situation in China. Hong Kong has the closest contacts with
churches in China. It may therefore be strategic to bring
the evangelical churches of Hong Kong together, so that
they will become the channel for sending Christian workers
back to China. Their counterparts in China would then
become the welcoming churches in China. If this is too
idealistic then :

ii. *A joint approach should be made to the Church in
China by a representative body abroad to arrange for the
return of selected Christian workers.* But, in this case, the
Chinese church organisation would need to be fully representative of all sections of the Church in China and the
negotiating body also fully representative of those organisations with the greatest interests in China. Not everybody
would accept the actual proposals made by a Roman Catholic bishop during a lecture in the U.S.A. but in principle
he is right in saying : "I believe that when the day for re-
newal of contacts with Chinese Christians does arrive it
should not be through the medium of either mission boards
or through national mission-sending societies. I would hope
that such contacts would be renewed by a supra-national
group . . . . The contact would best be made by a neutral,
non-national group. And I would hope that by the time

the mainland is opened to missionary activity again, the
ecumenical movement will have moved forward to such a
stage of development that the Gospel shall be preached
without the duplication of efforts and the outright competi-
tion which exists in many countries today." There is wisdom in these words, but they also indicate some of the
delicate problems which may complicate the return to
China, especially for those potential missionaries—the
majority in fact—who are not associated with the World
Council of Churches. Nevertheless, something of this kind
is surely essential to prevent the unfortunate confusion
of the pre-Communist era. Even if evangelicals do find it
impossible to cooperate with those who preach 'another
Gospel', it should not be too difficult to agree about a common policy among themselves.

iii. *Before any concrete programme is formulated, the
first step must be to seek the fellowship of the churches in
China.*

The gap in fellowship has been wide and long. It will
require time to renew close fellowship in Christ. Mutual
misunderstandings will need to be sorted out and criticisms
confessed. Humility will be essential for both sides. We who
have known nothing of persecution under Communism
will need to sit at the feet of Chinese Christians and share
the lessons God has taught them through suffering. They in
turn will hunger for the comfort of the Scriptures, having
been without Bibles and starved of a Biblical ministry for
so long. Furthermore we would be dependent on them to
interpret the new situation in China and to advise about
the gigantic task of reaching seven hundred to eight hundred million Chinese with the Gospel. To rush in with our
own schemes and to ignore or bypass the sorely wounded
Body of Christ in China would be to court failure.

iv. *In conference with the Church it would soon be
evident that there can be no thought of reverting to the pre-
1948 situation.*

The Gospel has not changed, but some of the methods
formerly used to proclaim it would almost certainly be
unacceptable. The familiar techniques and evangelical jargon
would cut little ice with a generation that knows only Marx

and Mao. Some methods might be borrowed from Communism, which originally borrowed and adapted its
methods from Christianity. It would be as essential to im-
part an understanding of the Bible as Communists now
instil the *Thought of Mao*. Mr. Watchman Nee, when he
and his colleagues met several leaders of the China Inland
Mission in Shanghai in 1951, was asked in what capacity
we should return if the doors of China were ever to reopen.
Without hesitation he said, "As teaching elders in our
churches!" He explained that evangelism will best be
done by the Chinese themselves but that Bible teaching in
the churches is a ministry for which our experience and
scholarship equip us. Manifestly, literature production and
broadcasting would play a major part as far as permitted,
but even these would need to be geared to the needs and
patterns of the New China.

v. *It will be essential to come to grips with the Communist ideology so as to communicate the Gospel relevantly
and powerfully.*

Evangelists have sometimes imagined that preaching the
Gospel consists merely in repeating (usually in occidental
thought form) certain doctrines about God, man, sin, the
Cross, faith, heaven and hell. But to a Muslim, a Buddhist,
a Hindu these either appear to be the same themes that
they are talking about only in an Eastern way or they seem
like strange tales of a foreign religion—interesting, but not
nearly so satisfying as their own religions. An approach
to Communists would be fraught with similar problems.
They are concerned with this world, not the next; with
poverty, hunger and injustice, not with sin; with the body,
not with the soul. At a recent conference in Malaya, group
discussion among young Chinese Christians revealed how
little even they knew about witnessing to those in their own
country of a different faith. So a much deeper study of
Communism than the outlines provided in Chapters IV
and V would be essential in order to appreciate the fallacies
and vulnerable areas in Marxism. The Christian must be
prepared for debate, dialogue, discussion as he seeks to
bring conviction to minds prejudiced against Christian
truth. But are we prepared for all that this demands of us

intellectually and spiritually? A merely negative anti-Communist attitude would only antagonise and would fail to open stony hearts and darkened minds to the Gospel. Members of the task force, besides being well-trained in Christian apologetics and Marxist dialectic, will also need to be Spirit-filled men and women if they are to match the deception-filled minds of the Chinese masses.

vi. *It will be essential to proclaim not the half truths and doubting assertions some have propagated in the past, but the positive certainties of the Christian faith.*

To introduce the theological doubts and current nebulous theories which are plaguing our Western churches and emptying both pews and pulpits, would be disastrous. To match the positive assertions and deep convictions of Marxists, Christians must proclaim a positive, authoritative, uncompromising Biblical message. Christian liberalism has a totally inadequate message for the world, particularly the Communist world. God must be shown to be alive, not dead. Christ must be proclaimed as the Lord of the universe and the unique Saviour of mankind.

vii. *Among young converts it might be helpful to adopt the small group or cell type of meeting so familiar to Communists.*

Even before Communism came to power in China, Christian students in Peking were aware of its techniques and some of their leaders used to hold self-criticism meetings at which frankness in sharing was required of all. So long as the dangers were recognised this Communist practice could be adapted to the needs of Christians in bringing about fellowship at a deep level. Christian fellowship must be more than a match for the ardent comradeship in a Communist society, as in fact it was among Christian university students in many universities in the brief post-war and pre-Communist era.

viii. *We would have to accept simple standards of living, avoiding the self-indulgence of the past.*

It should be unnecessary to say that mission boards must make no attempt to recover their old compounds, homes and institutions. In a socialist society, it would be intolerable to display the exclusiveness, aloofness and superior wealth, or to indulge in the luxuries and insist on the conveniences to which we were once accustomed. Those returning to work with the Chinese churches must go prepared to accept the accommodation and the conditions provided by the churches. The new generation of missionaries will be expected to be content with spartan simplicity of living and to seek a close relationship to the people.

ix. *It may be advisable for missionaries, like the Apostle Paul, to engage in some wage-earning occupation.*

The old image of the missionary as seen by the nationals was not very flattering : wealthy, comparatively idle, rather superior and aloof, and unwilling to soil his hands with things that servants were employed to do. Those who return to China may need to combine the preaching of the Gospel with some practical expression of social concern in a developing society. Mission hospitals are a thing of the past in China, but doctors and nurses could serve in state institutions. There will never again be mission schools or universities, but school-teachers, agriculturalists, engineers, social workers and university lecturers may find a welcome in government employ. One thing is certain : Christian workers of the future will need to be wise as serpents and harmless as doves.

x. *Those preparing for a re-entry into China must be ready for sacrifice as well as service.*

An article in *Floodtide* by Herbert Kane entitled 'Conflict Is Inevitable', says, "The Christian Churches must be prepared to beat the Communists at their own game — to outdo them, out-dare them, out-live them and, if necessary, out-die them!" On the 150th anniversary of the Bible Society, Professor James Stewart of Edinburgh preached the anniversary sermon in Westminster Abbey before the Queen and Prince Philip. His theme on that great occasion was that, in face of the present pagan threat to the world the effete, formal, traditional Christianity of today is useless. The anti-Christian forces abroad can only be met by the power of the Word of God and by Christians with such a faith in its truth, so convinced that they are right that they will be prepared, if necessary, to die for their faith.

If as Christians we had half the dedication and enthusiasm

of China's Red Guards we could again 'turn the world up-side down'. Men and women of this calibre will be needed to return to China—a China that has had its old foundations torn up only to discover that atheistic Communism has nothing to offer, nothing to satisfy the empty hearts of men, nothing to fill the vacuum it has created. The Chinese, like the rest of us, were made by God and for Him. If they knew, they would cry out :

Thou, O Christ, art all I want,
More than all in Thee I find.

CHAPTER X

CHALLENGE OF COMMUNISM

In an earlier chapter we have tried to show that Communism is a pseudo-religion, a subtle counterfeit of Christianity. It possesses many of the characteristics of the early Church which have long disappeared from modern Christianity. Could it be that the extent of the success of the Communist movement during the last fifty years is the measure of the Church's failure? At the risk of some repetition, the several ways in which Communism is a challenge to Christianity may serve to provide a summary of the subject.

The Challenge of its Idealism

The driving force behind Communism is its fiery hatred of conditions in the world as they are and a fervent belief that the perfect human society is an attainable ideal. The true Communist is a man with a passion for social justice. And he is fortified in his assurance by his belief in a natural law which is propelling mankind inevitably toward its Utopian goal—the law of Dialectical Materialism or economic determinism. In that Utopian era he looks forward to perfect justice, the end of the weary class struggle, the abolition of war, abundance for all, the unveiling of nature's last secrets, the final conquest of disease, the perfection of human nature and the dispensing with police forces and all forms of coercion. The concept is dazzling and especially so to people groaning under bad government, corrupt officials and unjust economic systems.

But why has the world not heard about the Christian goal—the rule of Christ on earth? Is it because Christians only half believe in it? Why have we allowed the Jehovah's Witnesses to steal our thunder? Isaiah and the other prophets spoke about the coming Kingdom in glowing terms. The Apostle Peter foresaw "new heavens and a new earth wherein dwelleth righteousness". And our Lord taught us to pray "Thy Kingdom come, Thy will be done on earth as it is in heaven!" Does not Communism challenge us to speak more clearly about Christ's personal return and the Kingdom He will then set up on earth?

The Challenge of its Dynamism

A Christian representative of a famous British chemical firm was one of a team that visited Peking on business in 1966. He gained a profound, almost terrifying impression of a nation throbbing with immense activity and with a strong sense of direction. The people were working with enthusiasm because they felt that they knew where they were going. Already China has succeeded in ending the disgrace of its former backwardness and in twenty years has made enormous strides materially. Despite frequent mistakes and serious setbacks, progress has been maintained and its evidences are there for all to see. Under a dynamic leadership with amazing organisational efficiency, the Chinese people are revolutionising their own country in every way. Economically they are rapidly catching up on the rest of the world. One goal they have set themselves is to overtake Great Britain in steel production by 1975. The experts believe that China, with its huge population, great skills and vast natural resources could become the world's greatest exporter long before the end of the century.

If Christians had the same sense of direction and half the dynamic enthusiasm in the attainment of their objectives, there would be no need to bemoan the declining church membership in Britain and the dwindling offers for overseas service. Christians today can hardly be described as those 'who have turned the world upside down'. But Communists can! An ideal Christianity has nothing to learn from Communism, but a decadent, orthodox Christianity bearing small resemblance to the Christianity of the New Testament must face the challenge of a militant Communism—and it is well for Christianity itself that the challenge should be faced and met.

The Challenge of its Materialism

This world is all there is, says the Marxist. Man is a body without a soul. Death is the end. Thus man's needs are confined to his bodily, social and cultural needs—food, sex, a home, work and profitable leisure. Satisfy these needs and all man's needs are satisfied. Man lives by bread alone. It is not difficult to imagine what it is like to be a Christian living in such an atmosphere, knowing as he does that man does *not* live by bread alone, that he and all his fellow men have undying souls for whose salvation Christ has died. Others around him look on the things which are seen. He fixes his attention on the things which are unseen and eternal (2 Cor. 4 : 18). So it is desperately difficult to maintain a Christian faith in a materialist and atheist society.

Here the challenge to us in Britain seems to be that the majority of our people, though not theoretical or philosophical materialists, are nevertheless practising materialists. God is not real. The soul does not seem to matter. All that matters for most of us is food, sex, a home, work and leisure to enjoy oneself according to choice. The danger is that, having adopted materialism as a way of life, we have yielded our first line of defence against Communism. If now it can be shown that a Socialist (Communist) government can order our material lives more efficiently than any other system, then why not let it? Humanists, unlike Christians, have no objections on religious grounds to Communism though they may fear its tyranny. The challenge to Christians therefore is so to live as to make it plain that, unlike their neighbours and colleagues, their main concern is not with material prosperity. Their heart's affections are firmly set on things above, not on things on the earth (Col. 3 : 2).

The Challenge of its Atheism

In the last twilight of the Nationalist regime in Peking, the writer was engaged in a discussion with a group of students in Peking University on the subject of 'ultimate reality'. It is easy for the Christian to give the glib answer "God is ultimate reality". But to a Communist, trained to think in terms of a materialist universe, the answer is not convincing. Marx and the early Communist prophets rejected God as a presupposition and built up a philosophy on His non-existence. Indeed, religion and belief in God were declared to be a positive obstacle to the attainment of the Communist goal. "Religion is the opium of the people," said Marx, drugging them so that they can be persuaded to be indifferent to the social injustices and to do nothing about changing the situation. Communists therefore are never tolerant towards religion : by definition they are militant atheists. Thus the 'ultimate reality' is not found in the sphere of religion, much less in the existence of a hypothetical God, but in the dialectical process which is ensuring human progress towards the perfect society. According to this theory the universe is not theo-centric but anthropocentric. Man himself is the centre of the universe.

How does a Christian meet this challenge? He should be able to match the philosophical argument with arguments of his own. In 1 Peter 3 : 15, we are told to be "ready always to give an answer to every man that asketh" us for a reason for the hope we have. But ultimately the issue is not intellectual but experimental. How real is God to me? What experience of God do I enjoy? Have I proved His power in time of need—in sorrow, suffering and perplexity? Is my religious faith more than a comforting drug to me? Does my belief in God give me a practical concern for the world around me and its needs?

The Challenge of its Evangelism

The deep convictions, bold assurances and burning hatred of the Communist for social and political evils and the people responsible for them make him an ardent missionary. The Red Guards exemplified the tremendous fervour of which the young generation is capable when they sense the value of a cause. Michael Browne's impressions of his visit to Canton in 1967 are worth recording again :

"Mao is god, the Party is the Church and the 'crusade' evangelists these youthful Red Guards. *Quotations* stands as their inspired writings and the glory of world revolution and world communism 'heaven'. Unbelievers are 'revisionists' and 'class enemies' normally termed 'monsters and ghosts'. Propaganda methods closely resemble Christian 'campaigns' with street meetings, cottage services, tract distribution, testimonies and even tonic sol-fa chorus sheets ! . . . In the light of what we saw in China our conclusions are that nothing in current luxury-loving, evangelical Christianity in the West even begins to approach the fearsome zeal and spirit of self-sacrifice shown by China's politically inspired youth. Unless we Christians can show at least a similar dedication and conviction for the Gospel we profess, our message will make little impression on a generation so passionately committed to its flaming destiny."

These are hard words, but who can contest their truth?

The Challenge of its Puritanism

Communist ethics are pragmatic. The Communist does not believe in an eternal unchanging moral law. His ideas of right and wrong are entirely relative. Since the ethics of any particular era are the reflection of the stage reached in economic progress, it follows that ethical standards change from age to age. Essentially, that which furthers the cause of the Communist revolution is right and everything else is wrong. This may justify at some stages, the use of deception, lying, cruelty, murder and torture, but only in so far as they serve the end in view. These same things would be regarded as evil in other circumstances if they hindered the progress along the socialist road to Utopia. Indeed, Communists can be and are, especially in the early years following revolution, quite Puritan in their outlook. In China, for instance, prostitution, gambling and petty theft were early targets of the new regime, and in an amazingly short time Shanghai's notorious organized vice and gambling rackets disappeared. Such bourgeois evils as sexual promiscuity, divorce and juvenile delinquency were looked upon with scorn. In 1967, the Rev. Ian Thomson observed : "In the course of three crowded weeks among thousands of people in many different circumstances I saw not a single instance of immodesty or embarrassment. In these respects it is a healthy-minded and moral society. The youth of China are busy with revolution and all their burning desire to 'serve the people' was in striking contrast to the headline news in Great Britain about a 'love-in' at Woburn and mini-skirts in Moscow, both of which would have confirmed the Chinese in their estimation of the decline of purpose in the West."

The Cultural Revolution aimed at purging society from bad habits and wrong ways of thought. Old-fashioned Marxist theory has always reasoned that, since evil originates in a wrongly ordered society, it is possible to change human nature by changing man's environment. Capitalism being the root cause of all human sin, sin will disappear with the destruction of the capitalistic system. A capitalist society, they claim, encourages selfishness, while a socialist society ('each for all and all for each') encourages unselfishness. In the final perfect socialist world, man will outlive his selfishness and the perfect socialist man will at last make the ideal happy society a reality. A lovely dream, but also a tremendous challenge to the Christian community to demonstrate the revolutionary power of Christ's unselfish love in all human relationships and in practical attempts to grapple with the problems human sin has created. Only then will the Communist be convinced that Christianity really works. "By this shall all men know that ye are my disciples, if ye have love one to another" (John 13 :35).

Challenge of its Nationalism

A student at Woolwich Polytechnic recently challenged the writer during the course of a lecture on 'China Today' to prove the charge that Christianity and imperialism have been hand in glove to be false. It is impossible to disprove what, in Africa, has manifestly been the case. There, missions have been the handmaid of colonial governments whose generous grants have from the first maintained mission schools and hospitals. A better case could be made out for missions in China where foreign governments have never financed Christian institutions. But the mud still sticks and missions have much to live down.

Here the challenge to missions is surely to take our hands off the churches completely now, both administratively and

financially; to eschew our former attitudes of mind—
paternal and condescending; to seek a new approach to the
national churches of the world, offering them our skills
and experience in the spirit of humble service.

In China the Church will never again tolerate foreign
control. In Africa it is high time to insist that foreign
control must end at once if real Christianity is to survive in
that continent. Western patterns and traditions need to be
abandoned. India and Japan should be well able to develop
their own orthodox, yet Asian-style, theology. The Chinese
Church has perhaps begun to hammer out new expressions
of the unchanging Gospel relevant to a dynamic Socialist
society. Can other Chinese, Asian and Westerners, to whom
there may come the privilege of joining forces with the
Chinese Church in its evangelistic task, rid themselves of
a traditional, western-orientated form of Christianity, tied
to an alien culture, and help rebuild a Church in China
which will no longer be a 'foreign religion' but deeply
rooted in the life and soil and culture of China and offering
to the Chinese people the deep satisfaction which they have
not found in the materialist answers of Communism?

CHAPTER XI

CONFRONTATION

PRESIDENT SUKARNO of Indonesia may have coined the word *konfrontasi* to describe his opposition to the new state of Malaysia, but he did not originate the idea. In Revelation 12, Satan is seen pursuing a confrontation policy with the Church of Jesus Christ. We have already noted in the Preface that this is the theme of the whole Book of Revelation and indeed of all human history since the Fall of Man. But here the two wonders are described—the woman who bears a child and the dragon who seeks his destruction. The child is Christ, who will one day rule the nations (v. 5), but the child is also the Church. Just as Satan attempted to destroy the child Jesus soon after His birth, so Satan, as described in the Acts of the Apostles, attempted to destroy the Church soon after its birth at Pentecost by fierce persecution.

Throughout the world today—and nowhere more evidently than in China—the great red dragon confronts the Church of Christ. The agelong war in the heavenly places is speeding to its climax (v. 7). Satan the deceiver, confusing men with his specious ideologies and attractive cults, has been cast out into the earth as a defeated foe (v. 9, 10). He is filled with intense fury because he knows that he has only a short time left (v. 12) and is therefore intensifying his persecution (v. 13).

Times of increasing trouble lie ahead—"Woe to the inhabitants of the earth . . ."(v. 12). But this is the eve of victory for the Church—"Now is come salvation and strength and the kingdom of our God and the power of His Christ" (v. 10). The blood of the Lamb and the word of our testimony will give us victory—on one condition! ". . . they loved not their lives unto the death" (v. 11). In what may prove to be the fatal hour of the world's history, God is looking for those who are prepared, if need be, to make the supreme sacrifice—men and women who are rid of self-love and, loving the Saviour supremely, are prepared to obey Him at whatever cost to themselves.

APPENDIX

In 1950 there were 11,470 local churches throughout China, over 7,500 evangelistic centres and about one million baptised Protestant Christians. There were over two thousand ordained Chinese ministers and more than ten thousand five hundred evangelists. Forty-eight Theological Colleges and twenty-one Bible Schools were training thousands of students. There were also eighteen Christian universities and colleges and over seventy Christian hospitals.

Does anything remain today? Did the Church have any endurable qualities? Of what calibre really was the Christian Church in China? Like the professing Church everywhere it was mixed. There was much formality. Nominalism was too common. Liberalism and modernist theology had eroded the foundations very widely. But where churches were firmly rooted in a Biblical theology they were generally characterised by a deep devotion, a spirit of prayer, a love for the Bible, a willingness to live sacrificial lives, a zeal for evangelism, a warmth of Christian fellowship, a spiritually-minded leadership, an unusual ability to expound the Scriptures and a passionate devotion to Jesus Christ.

The writer can never forget the brief years in Peking among the students before the Communist occupation. The above characteristics were most marked among these ardent young people who numbered some two hundred and who well knew what they were facing in the future. Charles C. West ('Barnabas') of the Ecumenical Institute, Bossy, Switzerland, contrasted them with other student organisations in his book *Christian Witness in Communist China* (S.C.M.), "Christian liberalism turned itself easily, too easily, into Christian-Communist Liberalism in China. Christian Liberalism failed to recognise the depth of sin and hence the need of personal salvation, humility and curbs on social power. The most vigorous Christian life in Peking today lies not in the churches but in Inter-Varsity organised student groups and sects." The whole Church in China could be divided broadly into these divisions : liberalism with a low message of salvation and evangelicalism with a Biblical theology and a strong, clear message about sin and God's remedy in the atoning work of Christ. Has the 'spiritual party' (the abusive epithet given to evangelicals) survived, despite imprisonment, persecution (not least at the hands of fellow 'Christians'), banishment to labour camps, loss of employment, destruction of Bibles, closing of places of worship and systematic indoctrination designed to undermine and destroy their faith? No complete answer to such a question is at present possible. But from the trickle of letters that reaches the outside world we gain the impression of a remnant in China with a strong faith that will endure to the end and will emerge from the fires purified and strengthened to undertake its important role in the future history of the Church.

In 1960 large numbers of Chinese, oppressed in Indonesia, elected to return to China. Some wrote of their experiences:

Hainan. 1961

"Dear beloved brothers and sisters in Christ. Grace and peace from God our Father and our Lord Jesus Christ. I've just arrived from Indonesia, but there is no place here to worship God and glorify His name. My spiritual life is now very weak. Pray for us that there may be a plan for us to return to a place where there is a church that preaches the Gospel of Christ's precious Blood and that men may be delivered from death to life, so that we may see again God's care for us . . . This is my hope. Emmanuel."

Peking. 1961

"Dear Pastor : Although I was a good student in Indonesia, I failed my entrance exam to the university here because I am not sufficiently 'progressive' and still have religious thoughts. Now I know you were right to warn me not to come to China, but I cannot leave again. When we went to church in Tientsin, the pastor wept to see us come in. Only a few old ladies were there beside us."

Peking. 1964
"Dear Brother Te-hsing,

I was overjoyed to receive your letter. It is now almost four years since I left Indonesia. However, I know a little of your circumstances and that through the Lord's great love we are united by one spiritual life. From afar I wish you all His eternal peace, spiritual blessing and revival and a greater love for the Lord.

Those who have returned to this land have greatly changed. Some have even turned their backs on the Lord and His Truth. This causes me deep grief. But there is a small group among our ranks who are still strong and brave for the Lord and continue to walk with Him. Because of their faith they are triumphant.

Last summer I visited Shanghai and attended three churches. The situation in the Shanghai churches is more satisfactory than that of the Peking churches. The International Church had a choir of twenty strong. It is possible there are only two churches in the whole country that still have choirs. Yes, we loved to hear the choir sing and we listened with deep emotion.

With regard to my school. I am very satisfied with conditions here. Although my studies take up a lot of time, I am able to pray and read the Bible each day and sometimes attend church. I am gladly and willingly walking the Calvary road and bearing my cross for Him. It is only this kind of life which is fully satisfying and is not in vain. I also thank God for His power and protection in keeping me from joining the Communist Youth Corps. I know His reason for this, for if I had joined it would have meant that I would need to publicly deny my Lord before others.

Please pray for this weak brother. Emmanuel!"

Letters received during the period of the Socialist Education Movement.
Nanking. 1965
"Recently I brought a radio set. One day I received a preaching broadcast accidentally . . . For certain reasons, I

have forsaken meetings for several years. I am longing for the message and the preaching of the Gospel such as I hear from the broadcasts. Usually I just read the Bible and pray at home. I do not take part in any group activities. But, in my heart there is a real need for fellowship with other brothers and sisters."

Yunnan. 1965

"First I give you my greetings. I thank God for His loyal servants who daily send out the news of God's great love, grace and power and His provision for lost men revealed in the soul-saving Gospel. During this period of deepening night and approaching daylight, when men's hearts are filled with sin and pain, what sweet spring it is to listen to God's Word and the Gospel hymns. How consoling they are! I hope God's Word may be sent forth all the time all over the world to fall as rain on the parched lives of men so that they may stand firm always in the direction of Mount Zion. Amen!"

Letters received during the Cultural Revolution period.
Yunnan. 1966

"Dear Auntie : Daddy's letter said that you had prepared some Christmas cards for me but that he did not risk sending them, as the ones sent last year were confiscated. Never mind. God's Word is in our hearts and cannot be confiscated. We will keep on going forward in His footsteps. Please, Auntie, do not feel badly about this.

Did you have a happy Christmas? I kept the season in my heart. The day before, I went up to the hills and picked some lion grass and decorated my little home. And I sang the Christmas song we used to sing when I was small and memory recalled the Christmases you celebrated with all us children . . . And now some good news for you. Once when I picked up the radio, I chanced on a Gospel broadcast from abroad. There was singing, prayer and reading from the Scripture . . . Alas, I might not listen very long, and I did not understand the foreign language used. In the city where I live there is a woman who is a true believer and witnesses in her home. I go there constantly and she encourages me greatly. Whenever we see each other, we have a short time of worship. All her family believe. May the Lord grant His blessing to this small, small church and cause it to be a little light in this dark world. May you have peace . . ."

From a labour camp. 1966

"Sister in S. (his wife) is far from well and has great difficulty in bearing the heavy burden of the whole family. Her most painful feeling is that her husband is away from home. They are like widow and orphans in the sight of God. We should pray much for them that they may be enabled to stand firm. But do not write to her please, it might cause her to suffer more. I do not know when I could go home for reunion with the family. All is in God's hands."

From prison. 1967

"I am very well and happy. Please be of good cheer. My feeling is just the same as yours. You must be very glad to hear this. All things work together for good. Be of good cheer. I am much more precious than sparrows."

Canton. 1967

"We listen to the Voice of Friendship and are finding help from God's Word. Thank you. Many of us are experiencing the protection of the Heavenly Father. Please realise our difficulties and pray for our country and fellow countrymen. May we all be together in the love of God. Emmanuel!"

Christmas 1967

"Christmas and New Year will be coming soon. At this happy time may all our brothers and sisters enjoy a day of abundance, for this is what Our Lord brought down with Him. Here I must give thanks and praises for all power and glory belong to God for ever. You must be very busy writing scripts. I await your lovely broadcasts and the New Year message."

Canton. December 1967

"I listened to the Voice of Friendship broadcast on Christmas Day. I could not give any present to the Lord this year and no one sent me any gift. How lonely I feel. You people overseas must have a good time this year. Can you

please send me a Voice of Friendship calendar as a gift?
Thanking you in advance. May God give us all happiness."

Canton. January 1968

"Thank you for your letter and calendar. May I ask you a
question? I was baptised and became a Christian in 1966.
But I have never been to a church since I left Indonesia
because the churches are all closed. Is it true that Jesus
Christ has left me? This question frightens me because my
present circumstances cause me constantly to sin."

January 1968

"Your letter and beautiful 1968 calendar arrived safely.
Thank you. After reading your letter and the message from
God's Word on the calendar, my heart was filled with sweet-
ness, as if resting beside the still waters. My family think of
you. Many brothers and sisters in Christ know rest in their
hearts. Each has his own prayer request."

January 1968

"Your letter and that beautiful and meaningful calendar
arrived safely. After looking at them, it was like the joy and
comfort of hearing the Gospel. This letter brought bound-
less fellowship, sad memories and warm feelings. I cannot
thank you enough for your instruction. I only came to real
faith in the Lord in 1962, having been moved by the Truth.
I am still young and know only a little about the Truth and
the Way. I hope you can teach me so that I can understand
much more Truth . . . I finished Middle School in 1966, but
school has been closed for a year so I feel sad and depressed."

March 1968

"I greatly need this kind of help in solving the problem of
the basis for joy and happiness. Formerly I did not understand who Jesus was because I don't have much opportunity
to listen to broadcasts. Thus I did not fathom the Jesus
principle. So please send me a programme schedule in order
that I can understand and believe."

April 1968

"Whenever my spirits sink to a low level and my heart is
confused, the voice of God and the call of God constantly

quicken me again. He enables me to understand principles that are not clear and to understand the world around me better. I think that there is too much sin in the world and God is warning us . . ."

May 1968
"I collect Christmas stamps. Please send me the recent New Zealand issue. Whenever I think of all our brothers and sisters, I feel glad. There are many verses in the Bible I do not understand. Since 1964 we here have not been able to read the Bible. Most Bibles have been burned. Don't you think this is a pity? Time is up. Praying always. A student."

May 1968
"Your letter was received a long time ago. For various reasons I have not replied until today. Greetings to your family. Please tell people about our situation and ask them to pray to the One who knows our requests. Also give thanks that when we were passing through great difficulties the Lord preserved my faith, love and hope and kept us. He also brought to Himself some lost sheep, for they were His chosen.

But what troubles me is that recently there has been a lack of harmony and backbiting among Christians and in Christian families and a lack of a dispassionate attitude, generosity and the love which covers a multitude of sins. Even I often fall and in my weakness commit sin. I want to leave Egypt, the bitter place of defeat; indeed, for the last month, things have been a bit better, thank the Lord, who preserved me during those months of difficulties, Those who understand are plenty, but quite honestly among them are the sons of Adam who have fallen to an unimaginable extent. But for God's love they would be beyond redemption.

Secondly, in examining my own weakness, I can only trust in the One who has passed through the dark valley of this world trusting Him to bring me in through the gate of His promises and salvation and hope that at the very end He will receive my soul.

Dear brethren, I have already spent twenty-six summers and winters and drunk much bitter wine. But now I understand the meaning of the words 'do not be conformed to this world'. I have hidden in my heart much deep teaching and so my heart is not too disappointed. With Paul I wish to be able to say 'I have fought the good fight, I have finished my course . . .' All is in the Lord's hands. Unfortunately I have had to return my borrowed radio, but I can still study the Bible and sing songs in my heart. Please forgive the length of this letter and I hope one day to shake your hand in person. Emmanuel!"

May 1968

"On the 28th of this month I was delighted to receive your letter. It made me very happy indeed. I think that all the glory for this should be given to God. It is His power, His will that has linked us up together. None can resist or hinder His power and His will. Here let us sincerely praise the Lord who has made us unseen acquaintances. May our nearly begotten friendship become ever deeper and stronger.

You are right in saying that the surrounding powers of evil, the endless hardships, the stony pathway are all trials allowed by the Lord in order that our faith and determination should become all the greater. In our lifetime we have experienced not a few dangers and obstacles. In the past, several times I almost lost my faith and hope in the future. This was possibly because my spirit was too weak. Nevertheless, despite this, I am prepared to undergo much greater trials, because my sufferings are not to be compared with those suffered by the Lord Jesus. Moreover, my weak spirit must advance to the hammered out strength.

Friend, recently my spirit has been greatly depressed because I have seen in the neighbouring river numbers of corpses floating down stream from Kwangsi province. These people, young and old, women and children deceived by Satan, who have lost their lives have gone to a lost eternity. What can we do? Who ever prayed for them that they might be saved? Joy to you from God."

> They climbed the steep ascent of heaven
> Through peril, toil and pain
> O God to us may strength be given
> To follow in their train.

BIBLIOGRAPHY

A Christian Commentary on Communism, by Edward Rogers (Wyvern)

Christianity and Communism (1936), ed. by H. Wilson Harris of *The Spectator*

Christianity and Communism Today, by John C. Bennett (S.C.M.)

Christianity and Marxism, by D. R. Davies (Victoria Institute)

Communism and Christian Faith, by Lester de Koster (Erdmans)

The Heart, Mind and Soul of Communism, by Fred Schwartz

Mao Tse-tung, by Stuart Scramm (Pelican)

Asian Analyst

The Guardian

The Times

China Bulletin, Asia Department, N.C.C., U.S.A.

China Notes, Asia Department, N.C.C., U.S.A.

Problems of Communism, Washington, D.C., U.S.A.